# PSALM 91

## STUDY GUIDE

\*

*MAKE*

*it*

# *MEANINGFUL...*

*MAKE*

*it*

# *REAL...*

*MAKE*

*it*

# *MINE!*

**Psalm 91 Workbook**
Psalm 91: God's Shield of Protection

Copyright © 2007
Peggy Joyce Ruth Ministries
P.O. Box 1549
Brownwood, Texas, 76804
1-877-972-6657
**www.peggyjoyceruth.org**

ISBN #978-0-9708257-6-6

First printing, 2007
Second printing, 2010

Cover design by Marcus Stallworth of Dallas, Texas

With Special thanks to:
Jeanne Pearce, Snow Bacon, JoDitt Williams, Micki Pelkey, Roberta Wescott,
Anthony Sandoval, Major James Linzey, Jo Schum, Lynne Williams,
Katie Townsend, Kim Sumpter, and Andrea Verano

# TABLE OF CONTENTS

## INTRODUCTION:

## LESSON ONE: A SECURE PLACE

## LESSON TWO: WHAT'S COMING OUT MY MOUTH?

## LESSON THREE: TWO WAY DELIVERANCE

## LESSON FOUR: HIS WINGS ARE A MIGHTY SHIELD

## LESSON FIVE: I WILL NOT FEAR THE TERROR
### (FIRST CATEGORY OF EVIL)

# LESSON SIXTEEN: I BEHOLD HIS SALVATION!

# INTRODUCTION

**Testimony as told by Jennifer McCullough:**

*"Before leaving for East Africa in 1999, I was being discipled by Angelia Ruth Schum (Peggy Joyce's daughter), my college Bible study teacher. It was a crash course on everything you need to know before entering "the Bush!" I ran into her friend Donna Crow one night at church and she said, "You do know about Psalm 91, don't you?" When I said "No!" she shocked me when she stated, "Angie must HATE you if she hasn't told you about Psalm 91!"*

*I immediately confronted Angie, "Donna says you hate me…!" "Why, would you say that?" Angie asked me, surprised at the charge…*

*I repeated again the message that had just been imprinted on me, "Donna says that you must hate me because you are letting me go to Africa without knowing about Psalm 91! She said that you must want to get me killed!"*

*Donna does have a way of getting a person's attention, but later we would all find out how important Psalm 91 would be to me. I began intently studying the chapter and memorized it before I left…"*

This true story illustrates how people are discovering for themselves the importance of a very old covenant of protection. Although scholars are not sure if this psalm was penned by Moses or David or some other inspired Biblical writer, they often try to downplay its meaning to words of comfort rather than bold declarations of what we have available in God. However, as you begin this workbook, discover for yourself the relevance of the promises that are declared in this passage. The writer makes no apology for the bold assurance of the protection available for those who dwell in the *secret place*.

In recent history, the importance of the psalm has not been lost to us. If you read Corrie Ten Boom's work you will see it mentioned. Jimmy Stewart's archives note his father's gift before he left to fly combat missions in World War II. The museum of Laura Ingalls Wilder in Independence, Kansas, famous from the TV series *Little House on the Prairie,* has on display Laura's Bible where she hand-copied the psalm in the opening pages and made special notes listing the benefits of this psalm upon her life on the prairie.

This psalm is a covenant of protection written by the Holy Spirit for believers today to help them understand the protection that God provides. It is especially beneficial to missionaries, law enforcement officers, military personnel, those struggling with illness and those who know that God's word makes a difference in their lives. There is a great deal of history that can be found from those who have discovered the power of these verses and share them in their own personal testimonies.

Truly, it would be dangerous to live in this world without a working revelation of this psalm. And yet, there are entire churches who have NEVER heard one lesson on Psalm 91, and preachers who have preached a lifetime without ever preaching this passage. Can you hear what Donna's voice is saying to those in that church, "Your church must hate you if you have never been told about Psalm 91!" Donna does have a way of getting one's attention. This workbook is your opportunity to do an in-depth, personal study into a psalm that can literally save your life.

# How to Utilize this Workbook

In your hands is the ability to unlock a personal revelation of God's promises of protection. This workbook is designed to give you a deeper understanding of the covenant God has provided for believers based on the promises from Psalm 91. It provides many approaches to studying this psalm - in small groups or through personal study - and is based on the work of Peggy Joyce Ruth's research of Psalm 91 through her book *Psalm 91: God's Umbrella of Protection.*

Can there be a promise in the Bible that does not work in the life of a believer? According to scripture there are three reasons why this can happen:

1. **Not <u>knowing</u> Scripture.** Matthew 22:29 says "…you err, not knowing the scriptures…"
2. **Not <u>mixing</u> the scriptures with faith.** Hebrews 4: 2 "the word did not profit them…not united by faith."
3. **Not <u>doing</u> what you know to do.** James 1:22 says "*hearers only* merely deceive themselves…" *

We would never want this to happen to you. These pitfalls can be avoided. This workbook is designed to (1) Help you know your covenant, (2) Ignite faith in you regarding the promises of God, and (3) Help you discover ways to immediately apply it to your life.

You will need a copy of one of Peggy Joyce Ruth's books (<u>Psalm 91: God's Umbrella of Protection,</u> <u>Psalm 91: Military Edition</u> or <u>Psalm 91: God's Shield)</u> to be able to work through the questions. (When the questions are only directly related to the military book a notation (M/Military) has been made.)

Each lesson in this workbook includes anecdotes and stories to consider with fill-in-the-blank questions and projects to work as a group or individually. There are applicable parables or analogies to help you think through various life events, questions to initiate personal response to concepts and pertinent links to the next lesson.

*Make it Meaningful, Make it Real and Make it Mine* is a concept designed to help you apply Psalm 91 right where you are living. At the end of each lesson, there is a page for you to *journal your thoughts*. This page allows you to stop and think about what you have just read and reflect on that lesson. Let this page be a place to write notes to God, a covenant for your life, prayer requests, or anything that might have struck a chord in your heart from that particular lesson.

This book is designed to be worked through a 16 week study of Psalm 91. Due to time constraints, it may be beneficial to work specific sections or to combine lessons to study in a shorter time period. The objective is to work at your own pace and soak up all the revelation from each particular verse before moving on. Working at your own pace allows you to dig deeply into what God wants to show you personally through each passage. As you take your time without having to rush, you'll be developing a stronger relationship with God, not simply doing homework.

*Special Thanks to Rachel Burchfield. Ideas for portions of this page are taken from Rachel Burchfield's book "How to Study Your Bible: Foundations for Life", TBI: Also chart on page 141 has been adapted, as well.

# LESSON ONE: A SECURE PLACE
## READ CHAPTER ONE THEME: A PLACE OF SAFETY IS AVAILABLE

**READ PSALM 91:1:** "He who dwells in the shelter of the Most High will abide in the shadow of the Almighty"

### Points to Ponder

Read the anecdote below or choose a volunteer to read the story aloud to the group. Answer the following questions.

Dad had a secluded place on the lake near Brownwood where he would take us to fish for perch. One of these outings proved more eventful than most—turning out to be an experience I would never forget. It had been a beautiful day when we started out, but by the time we had finished our perch fishing and were headed toward the cove, everything changed. A storm came upon the lake so suddenly there was no time to get back to the boat dock. The sky turned black, lightning flashed, and drops of rain fell with such force they actually stung us when they hit. Then moments later we were pelted by large, marble-sized hailstones.

I saw the fear in my mother's eyes and I knew we were in danger. Before I had time to wonder what we were going to do, Dad had driven the boat to the rugged shoreline of the only island on the lake. Although boat docks surround the island now, back then it looked like an abandoned island with absolutely no place to take cover. Within moments Dad had us all out of the boat and ordered the three of us to lie down beside our mother on the ground. He quickly pulled a canvas tarp out of the bottom of the boat, knelt down on the ground beside us and thrust the tarp up over all five of us. That storm raged outside the makeshift tent he had fashioned over us. The rain beat down, the lightning flashed and the thunder rolled, but I could think of nothing other than how it felt to have his arms around us. There was a certain calm that is hard to explain under the protection of the shield my father had provided. In fact, I had never felt as safe and secure in my entire life. I can remember thinking that I wished the storm would last forever. I didn't want anything to spoil the wonderful security I felt that day—there in our secret hiding place. Feeling my father's protective arms around me, I never wanted it to end.

Although I have never forgotten that experience, today it has taken on new meaning. Just as Dad had put a tarp over us to shield us from the storm, our Heavenly Father has a Secret Place in His arms that protects us from the storms that are raging in the world around us.

That *secret place* is literal, but it is also conditional! In Psalm 91:1, God lists our part of the condition before He even mentions the promises included in His part. That's because our part has to come first. In order to *abide in the shadow of the Almighty*, we must choose to *dwell in the shelter of our Most High God*. Think about a time when you were in a safe place and compare this to the meaning of Psalm 91:1.

1. The secret place is _____ but it is also _____ .

2. What made her feel so protected during the storm and how is this example similar to what God does for us as Christians?



3. How do we abide *in the secret place and in the shadow of the Almighty?*



## MAKE IT MEANINGFUL:
### Life Application Questions

Write out Psalm 91:1.

_____

_____

_____

1. Why does the author's personal story of a childhood memory of a father's arms fit the first verse of Psalm 91 so well?



2. What feelings does she describe in that childhood memory?



3. Our Heavenly Father has a _____ _____ in His arms that _____ us from the storms that are raging in the _____ _____ _____ .

4. God's *Secret Place* is _____ and _____ ! Our part of the condition must come first. What is our part of the condition?

5. How do we *dwell* in the shelter of the Most High?

_____

_____

_____

6. The author asks the reader, "What might you call that place of refuge?"  She defines it as a

_____ .


7. When you think of *security* and *safety* and *protection*, what memory comes to mind?


8. Name some of the fears that you currently have: (This could be anything from being afraid of the dark, to being afraid that you are going to miss out on something fun, to being afraid to try new things, to fear of death, etc).

_____
_____
_____
_____
_____
_____


9. Look up the following words in a dictionary.  Then write the definition in your own words:

Dwell-_____
_____

Shelter-_____
_____

Abide-_____
_____

Literal-_____
_____

Security-_____
_____

Shadow-_____
_____

# MAKE IT REAL: SPENDING TIME IN THE SECRET PLACE IN A BUSY WORLD
## Life Connection Parable

Christian families come in all shapes and sizes. The Howard family stands out in my mind because each member of the family has his own *secret place* where he meets with God. The father met with other business men for a prayer breakfast, but each day on his drive to work he would spend the hour in worship and prayer to properly start his day. The stressed out and overworked mom had heard the story of John and Charles Wesley's mother who had so many children to care for she could never find much quiet time. So she would throw her apron over her head while she cooked. The Wesley children knew not to bother their mom when she was in her "secret place." Mrs. Howard would rise early in the morning and go to a special place for her time with God. And like Mrs. Wesley, she too would apply the apron technique to her own life to snatch bits of time throughout the day to enter the secret place when things got too hectic. The Howards had also trained their children to have a secret spot to meet with God—the son behind the couch and the daughter on the porch. When the children grew up they kept this custom. The daughter would write home from college saying that because of the constant flow of other students, the only place she could find to have her special time with God was hidden in the stairwell next to the fire alarm system. The son made time for walks with God alone in the woods away from the campus. Each member of the family testified to how much better his day would go when he had "his time" with God. Testimonies of answered prayer were abundant in this family and each would mention that time seemed to S-T-R-E-T-C-H when they gave the first part of their day to the Lord. It didn't take long to notice that each of the members of the family developed a very personal relationship with God, making the rewards of the secret place well worth the time investment.

1. Since all of Psalm 91 seems to hinge on finding that secret place with God, how has the

   Howard family's story challenged you to start a definite time where you meet with God?


2. What special location in or around your home can you make for your secret place for you and God?


3. How could a *secret place* help you get to know God better?


4. Would you describe your relationship with God as <u>deep and meaningful</u> or <u>casual and sporadic</u>?


5. Why should we develop good *secret place* habits early in life?


6. What's one area in your life you could give to God in order to make time for a *secret place*?

*Talk/Write about your "secret place" and any special experience you would like to share. Name some personal steps you can take to better dwell in the shelter of the Most High.*

# MAKE IT MINE: KEEP THE WORD BEFORE YOUR EYES
### Life Relevance Project

## Verse reference: **Deuteronomy 6:4-9**

The Jews have a custom of putting scripture in a little ceramic, glass or sterling silver tube, called a Mezuzah, by their door to remind them of the place of God's word in their life. Many times they will kiss the scripture as they enter. Since the car has been a place of travel one can also find Mezuzahs for the automobile with scripture and prayers for safety. We can follow this scriptural admonition by putting this important psalm in a place where we will see it daily...

## Well-Placed Reminders of Psalm 91

*display Bible opened to Psalm 91
*framed on office wall
*on a note on the car dash
*on your computer screen
*welcome mat at front door
*magnet on refrigerator
*note on bathroom mirror
*coffee mug inscription
*camouflage bandana scarves
  (see testimony in Military Psalm 91)
* bookmark
*_____

# Bible Interaction
(List other Scriptures that came to your mind which relate to this chapter)

For example: *Psalm 91: 1(God's shadow) and Acts 5: 15 (man's shadow)*

*What does the shadow concept based on these two verses mean to you personally?*
*#1  Shadows can be good.*
*#2  The concept of protection and healing with a direct reference to shadows*
*#3  The shadow came and went as Peter came and went.*
*This is a much stronger realization to know we are abiding permanently in His Shadow!*
*#4* _____

**Link to Last Week:** In the introduction we discussed how a college student who was going on the mission field was surprised to learn that going on a trip without the knowledge of Psalm 91 was putting her life on the line. *Are you, like Jen, facing a situation where it is imperative that you know Psalm 91?*

**Bait to Next Week:** Let's see how our __mouth__ plays a role in our protection.

## *Respond With Your Heart*

*What are the benefits of a secret place?* _____
_____
_____

*Am I dwelling in the secret place?* _____
_____

*How can I dwell deeper?* _____
_____

*What can I do to develop my intimacy with God?* _____
_____
_____

*Am I abiding at all times in this refuge and fortress?* _____
_____
_____
_____

# Journal

# LESSON TWO: WHAT'S COMING OUT MY MOUTH?
## READ CHAPTER TWO                    THEME: HEART AND MOUTH

**Read Psalm** 91:2 "I will say to the Lord, 'my refuge and my fortress, my God, in whom I trust.' "

## Points to Ponder

Read the anecdote below or choose a volunteer to read the story aloud to the group. Answer the questions that follow.

Corrie Ten Boom, a Dutch woman, famous for her underground work of hiding Jews in World War II, told this story of an Englishman in her book, *Clippings from My Notebook*:

*Used by permission of Corrie ten Boom Foundation*

Many people came to know and trust the Lord during World War II. One day an Englishman, who was held in a German prison camp for a long period of time, read Psalm 91. "Father in heaven," he prayed, "I see all these men dying around me, one after the other. Will I also have to die here? I am still young and I very much want to work in Your Kingdom here on earth." He received this answer: "Rely on what you have just read and go home!" Trusting in the Lord, he got up and walked into the corridor toward the gate. A guard called out, "Prisoner, where are you going?"

"I am under the protection of the Most High," he replied. The guard came to attention and let him pass, for Adolf Hitler was known as "the most high." He came to the gate, where a group of guards stood. They commanded him to stop and asked where he was going. "I am under the protection of the Most High." All the guards stood at attention as he walked out the gate. The English officer made his way through the German countryside and eventually reached England, where he told how he had made his escape. He was the *only one* to come out of that prison alive.

By actually quoting out loud from Psalm 91, God delivered the prisoner from a concentration camp. The man could have read the psalm and enjoyed it, he could have pondered the words and he could have thought about the meaning, but his deliverance came *when he actually started **saying** the words out loud!*

1. What are some areas where you are neglecting to speak God's Word out loud?

2. What could be different in your life if you started quoting God's promises out loud?

# MAKE IT MEANINGFUL:
## Life Application Questions

1. Write out Psalm 91:2 - _____

_____

_____

2. What phrase does the author highlight from Psalm 91:2?

3. There is _____ in _____ His Word back to Him! (Military)

4. We are not told to simply _____ the Word. We are told to _____ the Word.

5. An example from Joel 3:10 advises the weak to say, "_____."

6. What does the author say that great men of God in the Old Testament have done? (Military)

7. Psalm 91:2 makes the analogy of who God is; He is a _____ and a _____. (Military)

8. What happens when we confess our trust *out loud*?

9. By _____ His Lordship and His protection we _____ to the secret place.

10. Define Refuge - _____

11. Define Fortress - _____

12. What has to happen before the promises in Psalm 91 will ever work?

13. According to Psalm 60:11b, why does God have to be our source?


14. God has to be the One to whom we run _____.  He is the only One who has the answer for _____ might come.


15. When the author thinks of how utterly impossible it is to protect ourselves from all the evils in this world, what is she reminded of? _____

16. Why?


17. God wants us to see Him as our _____ of _____.
He is our _____.

18. Psalm 91 is powerful and it works simply because it is the _____ of _____, _____ and _____. (Military)


19. Define Active-_____


20. What happens as we allow God to be the Lord of our lives?


21. What prayer has the author learned to say out loud?


22. In times of trouble, what is the worst thing you can do? (Military)


23. Psalm 91 tell us to do just the opposite - _____ _____! (Military)

# MOUTH PROBLEMS

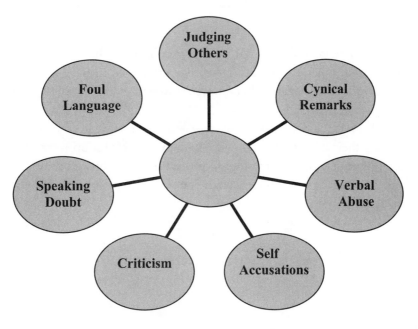

How many of these have you done this week?
Write the number in the center circle.

# MOUTH RESOLUTIONS

How many of these have you done this week? Write your answer in the center circle. Compare this number to the number of mouth problems.

# MAKE IT REAL: A TIME TO TRUST AND A TIME TO SAY IT!

Life Connection Parable

Kenneth longed to hear someone tell him that they trusted him. He had grown up in a home where few words were ever verbalized, especially anything positive. He hoped to have his parent's trust; but, if they did trust him, he was never aware of it. When he went through grade school he longed to be the one the teacher trusted with special privileges.

The first time Kenneth ever heard trust verbalized was in his first year of marriage. Late at night, suspecting someone was on their back porch, his wife, Tiffany, woke him up to tell him she had heard something. When she told Kenneth she trusted him to protect her, it resonated something deep inside of him. She had verbalized her trust in him, even though she was afraid. Kenneth felt strength come into him as he headed to that back porch…

1. Explain how Tiffany was able to verbalize trust when she was afraid.

2. The writer of the Psalm boldly tells God that he trusts Him! Have you ever told God in the midst of a threatening situation that He was your security and you trusted in Him?

3. How can verbalizing God's Word make a difference over just thinking it?

*Talk/Write about an experience where you realized God was your only source.*

# MAKE IT MINE: WHERE HAVE YOU PUT YOUR TRUST?
**Life Relevance Project**

## NATURAL CHECKLIST:
* Double check our cars to make sure the motor, tires and
  brakes are all working properly
* Fireproof our houses
* Store up food for times of need
* Open a large bank account to have money for rainy days
* Build storm cellars and nuclear bomb shelters
* Add the latest burglar systems to our home and cars
* Put burglar-proof locks on our doors
* Get immunization shots for every known disease
* Put 911 in the speed dial of every phone
* Have airbags installed in all our cars
* Hire the biggest and strongest person we know as a bodyguard

It is impossible in the natural to anticipate and cover every potential problem that might arise. But God has provided a thorough coverage in the spiritual realm. Just as you buy multiple layers of protection in a natural insurance policy to achieve a more thorough coverage, in the same way we can cover ourselves thoroughly by writing a Biblical insurance policy against any area that would try to attack our families. There are various scriptures from the Bible that promise protection for all the areas named above. Psalm 91 is unique because all the protection promises are summarized in that one chapter. Insurance policies may fail, but the Word of God will never fail!

## TRY THIS:

Try saying out loud, "Insurance policy/Bank account/Door Lock, I trust you!"
Now say out loud to the Lord, "Lord, you are my Refuge and my Fortress,
You are my God in whom I trust!"

Observe the difference in verbalizing your faith in God OUT LOUD...
Notice how it feels to openly proclaim your trust in an inanimate object (insurance policy, bank account, door lock) rather than a PERSONAL relationship with God.

*Don't you like having people tell you that they trust you?*
Remember that God enjoys hearing you **tell Him** how much you trust Him.

# Bible Interaction
(List other Scriptures that relate to this chapter)
Joel 3: 10, Psalm 60:11, John 10: 11, Jeremiah 29: 11, Psalm 118: 17

**Link to Last Week:** Don't forget the importance of that *Secret Place* that we talked about last week. Have you found yourself a special place to meet with God?

**Bait to Next Week:** We will be taking a closer look at the two-way deliverance (from temptation and physical danger) that God has made available (Military).

## *Respond With Your Heart*

*What area of my life do I need God's help to control my tongue?*

_____

_____

_____

*Am I deliberately speaking my faith when I am afraid?* _____

_____

_____

_____

*Am I speaking my trust to the Lord out loud?* _____

_____

_____

*In what area of my life can I choose to trust God more?* _____

_____

_____

*Have I ever spoken to a problem in my life using the authority of God's Word?* _____

_____

_____

# Journal

# LESSON THREE: TWO WAY DELIVERANCE
## READ CHAPTER THREE    THEME: SPECIFIC TRAPS AND GENERAL TRAPS

**READ PSALM 91:3**: "For it is He who delivers you from the snare of the trapper and from the deadly pestilence."

## Points to Ponder

**Read the analogy below or choose a volunteer to read the story aloud to the group. Answer the following questions.**

Have you ever seen a movie where a fur trapper travels deep into the mountains in the cold climate? He baits big, steel traps, covers them over with branches and then waits for some unsuspecting animal to step into the trap.   Those traps were not there by chance. The trapper has taken great care in placing them in very strategic locations.  In wartime a mine field is set up the same way.  Those land mines are methodically placed in well calculated locations.

These are pictures of what the enemy does to us. That is why he is called the *trapper!* The traps that are set for us are not there by accident.  It is as if the trap has your name on it.  They are custom made, placed and baited specifically for each one of us.  But like an animal caught in a trap, it is a slow, painful process.  You don't die instantly.  You are ensnared until the trapper comes to destroy you.

The enemy knows exactly what will most likely hook us, and he knows exactly which *thought to* put into our minds to lure us into the trap. That is why Paul tells us in *2 Corinthians 2: 11* we are *"…not to be ignorant of the schemes (traps) of the enemy."*

1. In what ways can you compare the enemy to a fur trapper?


2. How can we as believers avoid a similar trap in the future?


3. How can you predict or recognize when you are most in danger of falling into a trap?


4. What protection does Psalm 91 offer to us in regards to traps that usually have bait that entice us?

# MAKE IT MEANINGFUL:
## Life Application Questions

1. Write out Psalm 91:3 - _____

_____

2. In the movies, what is the objective of the trapper?

3. What had the trapper taken great care to do?

4. That's why the _____ is called the _____.

6. The traps that are set for us are not there by _____.

7. What does John 10:10 say?

_____

_____

8. The _____ knows exactly what will most likely _____ us, and he knows exactly which _____ to put into our _____ to lure us into the trap.

9. What did Paul tell us in II Corinthians 2:11?_____

_____

10. Who is the only one to deliver us from the snare of the trapper?

11. II Corinthians 10:4-5 says, "For the _____ of our warfare are not of the _____ but divinely _____ for the destruction of _____. We are _____ speculations and every lofty thing raised up against the _____ of God and we are taking every _____ _____ to the _____ of Jesus Christ."

12. What does God deliver us from in the last part of Psalm 91:3?


13. What things did the author name that she thought were pestilence?


14. After doing a word study on pestilence, what did the author learn?


15. What does God say about pestilence?


16. According to Matthew 10:16 we must: "Be as _____ as _____, but as _____ as _____." (Military)

17. What is the advantage of the combination of these two animals?


18. What two things are we delivered from?


19. How is this verse about traps comparable to a similar statement in the Lord's Prayer?

*Webster's New World Dictionary says that* pestilence *is "any virulent or fatal disease; an epidemic that hits the masses of people." A pestilence is any deadly disease that attaches itself to one's body with the intent to destroy." But God says that He will deliver us from the deadly disease that comes with the intent to destroy."*

20.  Name some examples of pestilence: _____
_____.

# MAKE IT REAL:   DELIVER US FROM EVIL!
Life Connection Parable

Clint had repeatedly fallen in the same area. It just seemed easier to give up and keep on sinning. What did it hurt to do it one more time when he had done it so many times before? Yet the confusion and disorder in his life was growing as the repercussions to his sin became more and more apparent. Clint was trapped in a vicious cycle of sin with growing consequences.

However, Clint's buddy, Andrew, listened to his friend's admission that he had almost given up on himself because he had fallen so many times. Andrew related a story he had heard growing up in church of a serial killer who had become a Christian. The Sunday school teacher had told his class how their sinning would begin to decrease as they spent more time with God. The serial killer rejoiced at the news that there was hope for his soul. He stood up the next week in his Sunday school class and gave the testimony that he had found what the teacher said to be true—that the progression of sin in his life had reversed. He stated with a note of triumph that he had cut back on sin, having only killed two that week!

Clint chuckled at the ridiculous analogy of the serial killer to his own life of repetitive sin, but he got the point. Andrew explained that the worst thing Clint could do was give up and keep sinning. Faith seemed to emerge in Clint's heart that it was possible to stop. Andrew shared a little secret with Clint, "Since childhood I have prayed the Lord's Prayer—Lord, lead me away from temptation and deliver me from harm." Andrew confessed, "It seemed at times that God just supernaturally would lift me out of the path of temptation. It wasn't that I was such a good kid, but my daily, fervent prayer to be led away from temptation actually cleared my path!"

1.  Why is it important to repent instead of continuing to participate in habitual sin?


2.  Why is sin attractive when portrayed by the world?


3.  How does spending time with God decrease our appetite for sin?

*Talk/Write about an experience in which God delivered you from a trap the enemy had carefully set for you.*

Author's Note: In this chapter there are two *Make it Real: Life Connections* because of the two-fold deliverance described in this verse. This covers the second aspect...

# MAKE IT REAL: HARM: ACCIDENT PRONE
Life Connection Parable

Kirk's life was noticeably accident prone from the beginning. At birth, Kirk had complications surrounding his delivery that were unlike any other the doctor had seen. This pattern continued. It was obvious to his parents from the time Kirk was small that he was accident prone. In fact, it became the household family joke that Kirk's dad could never afford to lose his job—not because of the paycheck, but for the insurance. Kirk had had so many repeated trips to the emergency room he was on a first name basis with the staff. His family gave Kirk posters for his wall that poked fun at his calamity, cut out cartoons related to Kirk's constant mishaps, and even give him calendars each year that related new sets of Murphy's Laws. However, as he got older, his escapes were becoming narrower and narrower.

When Kirk got married and had the responsibility of a wife and family, the many close calls he experienced in a week were no longer a laughing matter. Kirk had been raised in a Christian home, but no one thought of this as a spiritual attack on Kirk's life. Nor had his church ever taught Scripture from a practical application standpoint. Instead, he had been taught that the Bible was only a history book. Fortunately for Kirk, his wife was a relatively new believer and more practical in her approach to Bible stories. She was utterly horrified at her new husband's indifference to multiple broken bones, concussions, auto wrecks, snake bites, and general misfortune. She saw the testimonies in the Bible from a perspective that if God had done it once, He would do it again in their lives. It was actually like a fresh breath of air to Kirk when she challenged him to find a verse that would free him from this constant calamity. Kirk had been taught that victory over sin was the only deliverance from the snare of the enemy, never realizing that he was barely escaping the traps laid out for his life. There was more to this promise than Kirk had ever experienced!

1. How did Kirk's wife conclude his accident-prone behavior as a spiritual attack?

2. How could Kirk's pattern of disaster ruin his life?

3. In what ways can Kirk step out of this spiritual attack?

# MAKE IT MINE:    FORCING A TEST
Life Relevance Project

Jesus refused to use His power for selfish goals. This principle was shown to us in Matthew 4:1-11 when Christ was tempted to turn stones into bread, jump off the temple, and bow down and worship Satan. In fact, a portion of Psalm 91 comes up in this dialogue between Jesus and Satan. Satan tempts Jesus to use the power of Psalm 91 in an inappropriate way—to throw Himself off a building to challenge the authority of these verses.  Jesus refused to try and harm Himself to see if God would prevent it because of these promises. Jesus' answer showed the temptation for what it was—an attempt to test the Lord.  Yet, at other times in life we see Jesus walking in confidence of His protection.

On a chalkboard or on a sheet of paper make one column listing ways in which Psalm 91 can be appropriated in faith and another column listing ways in which the text could be twisted to be a test.

**Inappropriate Tests: (for example)**
--An attempt to shoot at a person to see if that person's shield works
--A challenge for someone to raise every sick person in a hospital to prove that God heals…
--_____

**Appropriate Applications: (for example)**
--A missionary life is threatened and the missionary continues to work, knowing that
   God has personally assured him of protection.
--A person prays for a friend's healing according to James 5, Mark 16
--_____

**Additional Applications of the distinction between "forced tests" and "applying promises":**

1. What is the difference between *turning stones* into bread when He was hungry and Jesus breaking the bread to feed the hungry?

_____
_____
_____


2. What is the difference between Satan's telling Jesus to jump off the temple because the scripture declares that the angels would bear Him up lest He dash His foot against a stone and Jesus' declaration that He had legions of angels available to Him at His disposal for protection?

_____
_____
_____

**Romans 3:23 tells us all have sinned and come short of the glory of God.**

**On this scale from 1 to 10, circle the number that signifies how much sin is controlling your life right now (with 1 being "not at all" and 10 being "relentlessly").**

| 1 | 2 | 3 | 4 | 5 | 6 | 7 | 8 | 9 | 10 |

**Proverb 6:18 tells us "one" of the seven things God hates is feet that are quick to run to sin. In your prayer time, thank God for sending His Son through whom we can be set free from sin.**

Name three Biblical ways to overcome a specific sin that you are facing:

_____

_____

_____

# Bible Interaction
(List other Scriptures which relate to this chapter)
2 Corinthians 2:11, 2 Corinthians 10:4-5, Matthew 10:16,
Matthew 6:13, Matthew 8: 16-17

**Link to Last Week:** As a reminder from last week's lesson—the way to appropriate faith is always 'Heart and Mouth'—believing with the heart and confessing with the mouth!

**Bait to Next Week:** This protection is not automatic for the Christian. Even though it is promised, there are some conditions to receiving the promises. In next week's lesson we will study a real life story that the author witnessed of a hen and her chicks and a hawk, and how to make sure we are under the wings!

## *Respond With Your Heart*

*What influences has the snare of the trapper had on my life?*_____
_____
_____

*What choices do I have in response to sin?* _____
_____
_____

*How can we as Christians help each other avoid the enemy's traps?*
_____
_____

*How can I decrease the amount of sin in my life?* _____
_____

*Am I convinced that I am delivered from the deadly pestilence?*_____
_____
_____
_____
_____

# Journal

# LESSON FOUR: HIS WINGS ARE A MIGHTY SHIELD
## READ CHAPTERS FOUR-FIVE
Theme: Protection in the Form of Wings and a Shield

**READ PSALM 91:4:** "He will cover you with His pinions, and under His wings you may seek refuge. His faithfulness is a shield and a bulwark."

### Points to Ponder

Read the anecdote below or choose a volunteer to read the story aloud to the group. Answer the questions that follow.

My husband Jack and I live in the country. One spring our old mother hen hatched a brood of baby chickens. On a particular afternoon when they were scattered all over the yard, I suddenly saw the shadow of a hawk overhead and noticed something very unique that taught me a lesson I will never forget. The mother hen did not run to those little chicks and jump on top of them to try to cover them with her wings. No!

Instead, she squatted down, spread out her wings and began clucking. And those little chickens came running from every direction to her to get under those outstretched wings. Then she pulled her wings down tight, tucking every little chick safely under her. To get to those babies, the hawk would have had to go through the mother.

When I think of those baby chicks running to their mother, I realize it is under His wings that we may seek refuge— but we have to run to Him. "*He will cover you with His pinions, and under His wings, you may seek refuge*" (New American Standard). That one little word "may" is a strong word! It is up to us! All that mother hen did was cluck and expand her wings to tell them where to come.

1. How are we as Christians similar to those baby chicks?

2. How is God similar to the mother hen in this story?

3. What is the significance of the word "*may*" in verse 4?

*Author's note: Special thanks to artist Jose Carlos from Brazil, for his artwork illustrating our story in* <u>My Own Little Psalm 91 Book</u> *written for young children!*

# MAKE IT MEANINGFUL:
### Life Application Questions

1. The promise in Psalm 91 is not elaborating on the _____ wing - but on the _____ wing.  One indicates _____ and _____, while the other indicates_____ and _____. (Military)

2. What word in this verse is highlighted? _____

3. What does "*may*" mean?

## Hen and Chicks and Hawk

*Author's note: Special thanks to Brownwood artist David Phillips for his illustration of the author's story of the hen and chicks in Psalm 91 for Youth!*

4. What picture did God give the author to illustrate this verse?

5. What happened while the chickens were scattered all over the yard?

6. Did the mother hen run to the chicks?

7. What did the mother hen do?

8. What did the chicks do?

9. How does this relate to us and God?

10. God is deeply _____ to us – yet at the same time, we can _____ His outstretched arms if we so choose. It is _____, not _____. (Military)

11. What happens when we run to God in faith? (Military)

12. Write out Psalm 91:4 _____
_____
_____

13. God's faithfulness is compared to what? _____

14. How can we ward off the enemy's attacks?

15. According to a Bible dictionary, what is a bulwark?

16. Why do some people feel that they can't *dwell in the shelter of God?*"

17. What have they forgotten?

# CLUES TO A MYSTERY
## REBUILDING THE BRIDGE TO A WWI PSALM 91 STORY

> A "miracle" regiment in World War I went through some of the most intense and bloodiest battles without a single combat injury. The story says that both officers and enlisted men quoted the 91st Psalm together and the entire group of soldiers did not have a casualty.

# Imprinted on shell: Argonne 1918
# St. Mihiel 1918

**Latest Clue in our search:** Marian Jones from Arkansas sent us these photos of cannon shells, souvenirs from her father, Lt. Harry McGee Cooper, who served in WWI. Those shells had been on the mantle for as long as she could remember. After Marian inherited the shells, she was cleaning them and found **the popular version of the World War I "Psalm 91 testimony" citing Argonne, etc.** (matching the embossed cannon artillery inscription) typed and wedged deep inside the shell. **Who put that story inside that shell?** Harry died when Marian was 15. Her mother had also passed on, so questions were left unanswered. *Yet, in our search, at every dead end, clues continually appear that open new doors to explore in rebuilding the bridge to the basis of this story... (Chapter 5: A Mighty Fortress Is Our God, Military Book, Psalm 91:4b)*

## CAN YOU HELP US WITH THIS SEARCH?

# THE TRAIL OF THE WWI REGIMENT...

**Katherine Pollard Carter**, a journalist, recounts in her book, <u>Mighty Hand of God</u>, (pages 31-32) this same WW I Psalm 91 story and gives us another clue that the story was published in periodicals on both sides of the Atlantic.

Katherine Pollard Carter references this WW I story in the writing of Will Ouhsler (Oursler) in American Weekly. 1958. Vol 21.

Katherine Pollard Carter died in 1989 without children, and we located her estate after months of research, only to find that thirty boxes of research and files that Carter had used to write her book had been disposed of months before in the Baytown city dump. Seven boxes of materials from the estate, left to the UT library in Austin, Texas, were carefully searched for clues. This find of laborious historical research only validated in our minds what careful documentation Carter made before publication of her stories. History was lost when those boxes of research were discarded.

F.L. Rawson, a British scientist, in his book, <u>Life Understood</u>, wrote about the WW I British brigade which had no casualties after claiming Psalm 91 as a unit.

Antique postcard: There is a safe place to hide and it featured this story. (Date was illegible)
Merit publications, Dept. S-7, 300-4<sup>th</sup> Ave., New York, 10, NY
(It was addressed to a resident in Doniphan, Nebraska, with a penny postage stamp on the card.)

[Businessreform.com] Internet
The story has been disputed because of confusion regarding some of the facts. Here is a review, clarifying some of the issues of the dispute. Pastor Robert H. Reid on July 8, 2006, "...regarding Larry Klass' comments (stating there was no 91<sup>st</sup> brigade), this is true if you are referring to the U.S. Army. However, the 91<sup>st</sup> Brigade was a composite brigade put together in England. **The story is true and it refers to a British unit, not an American**."

**Other wars have similar stories regarding Psalm 91, the soldier's psalm, which have been adequately researched and documented.**
We hope to rebuild the bridge for this WW I story as we continually look for clues of its origin... Somewhere, out there in letters, books or museums, lie the rest of the facts and documentation to this famous story.
www.peggyjoyceruth.org

# MAKE IT REAL: UNSEEN SHIELDS
Life Connection Parable

In the Military Psalm 91 book, the author relates a story of a British chaplain who lay exposed on the sandy beach of Dunkirk. The Nazi bombers flew over his body which was in plain view, dropping their bombs and firing their machine guns—kicking up sand all around him.

Although dazed by the moment, he suddenly realized he had not been hit by any of the bullets raining down on him. But, what amazed him more was when he stood up—the outline of his body was in the sand and it was the only smooth and undisturbed spot on the entire bullet-riddled beach. His heavenly shield must have fit the exact shape of his body that day.

1. Do I take the scriptures about my shield of protection literally enough?

2. Think of a story in *your own life* or *someone you know* where God was a literal shield of protection:

3. What are the natural circumstances of this testimony that determine it could have only been a supernatural deliverance?

***Talk/Write about the reality of this invisible shield in your own life.***

# MAKE IT MINE:   GOD IS NUMBER #1 IN MY LIFE!

### Life Relevance Project

## Hours In a Day

With 24 hours in a day we all make choices of how to spend them. The normal tasks of daily life such as eating, sleeping and work consume the majority, but *how often do you spend leisure time growing in God?* List the other tasks you engage in daily and how much time they consume.
*Is your time balanced? Does it reflect the importance of God's will?*

24 HOURS in a DAY
__ hours asleep
__ hours eating
__ hours spent at work
__ hours driving
__ hours of exercise
__ hours watching TV/entertainment
__ hours with family
__ hours praying
__ hours reading the Bible
__ hours spent in service to others
__ other _____

| 18 | Monday |
|---|---|
| **To Do:** | |
| laundry | |
| shopping | |
| groceries | |
| homework | |

**HINT: IF YOUR NUMBERS ADD UP
TO MORE THAN 24 ... START OVER !**

# PRIORITIES

How much time each day do you spend preparing spiritually for your day?

How much time do you spend memorizing scriptures on protection?

Do you take the time to remind yourself each day that God is literally a shield to your life?

At night, do you take the time to reflect on God's protection during your day and to thank Him?

Is there a time you actually read the 91st Psalm to yourself?

## Bible Interaction

(Other Scriptures which relate to this chapter)
Isaiah 40:31, Matthew 23: 37,  2 Timothy 2:13, Ephesians 2: 8-9,
1 Corinthians 1: 30

**Link to Last Week:**  God offers us deliverance from both sin-traps and diseases.

**Bait to Next Week:**  Next week we will be talking about the portion of Psalm 91 which covers a promise of protection from every evil known to man.

## *Respond With Your Heart*

*How can I let God's shield become more of a reality in my life?* ___

_____

_____

_____

_____

*Has my heart pondered the protection of a shield?* _____

_____

_____

*Name as many Bible verses as I can that relate to a shield:* _____

_____

_____

_____

_____

_____

# LESSON FIVE: I WILL NOT FEAR THE TERROR
## READ CHAPTER SIX          THEME: THE FIRST CATEGORY OF EVIL

**READ PSALM 91:5A**: "You will not be afraid of the terror by night..."

## Points to Ponder

Read the anecdote below or choose a volunteer to read the story aloud to the group. Answer the following questions.

Joann was in my first college Bible study group. I had been teaching Psalm 91 and reiterating the four categories of evil: 1.) terror (evil that comes through what another person can do to us: robbery, murder, rape, terrorism, kidnapping, etc.), 2.) arrows (assignments deliberately sent by the enemy to wound us), 3.) pestilence (deadly diseases), and 4.) destruction (natural disasters like tornadoes, floods, car wrecks, etc.) I had spent some time emphasizing the fact that rape comes under the heading of *terror by night* and God had very plainly said that we were not supposed to fear the terror—it would not approach us if we dwell in the shelter of the Most High and run to Him for protection.

It was several weeks later that a man forced Joann's car off the road one night and jerked her out of the car with the full intention of molesting her sexually. She said that her knee-jerk reaction was to scream at the top of her lungs for help, which she did, to no avail. But as he was ripping off her clothing the words of Psalm 91 came back to her—*You will not be afraid of the terror by night. It will not approach you!* She quit screaming for help and started quoting that promise over and over. Suddenly, he threw her down, *shouted*, "I would get a religious freak," and took off in his car without carrying it any further. She later told me that all of her screaming was no deterrent whatsoever, but the moment she began declaring her covenant promises, he left.

1. If Joann had continued to cry out in the natural what do you think would have happened?

2. This story is an example of how important it is to know what your covenant is before you get into a desperate situation. How well do you know your covenant?

3. Is there something that you have greatly feared happening to you?

# MAKE IT MEANINGFUL:
### Life Application Questions

1. Write out Psalm 91:5a _____
_____

2. Using a dictionary, write the definition of terror: _____
_____

3. Verses five and six encompass _____.

4. What is the first category of evil covered by this text?

5. What does it include?

6. God says not to be afraid of terror because_____.

7. Why did Jesus tell us repeatedly that we should not be afraid?

8. What is fear the opposite of? _____

9. What does fear keep us from doing?

10. How does fear come about?

11. Why is this wrong?

12. Faith is simply the _____ to _____ what Jesus has _____ done.

13. What is our better protection?

14. How do we activate this protection?

15. It is _____ and _____ - believing with our _____ and confessing with our _____.

16. Our physical weapons are operated with our _____, our spiritual weapons are operated with our_____.

17. How is the Blood applied?

18. Fear comes in when we are _____ things other than what God has said.

19. II Corinthians 5:7 instructs us to "_____."

20. Just as the law of aerodynamics can supersede the law of gravity, Satan's attacks can also be superseded by a higher law-the law of _____ and _____ to God's _____.

**FEARLESSNESS** —Verse 5 says, "you will not be afraid of…" and names the four categories of evil.
The *fear of terror* has to be dealt with because fear opens DOORS!
**Terror by Night:** Evil that comes by man: Murder, War, Rape, Kidnapping, Night-time Crimes.
God doesn't promise a world FREE FROM DANGER…but PROTECTION in it!

## True or False?

_____If I can just believe hard enough, I will be protected.
_____Faith is just the choice to receive what Jesus has already done.
_____God promises to protect us from every evil, except terrorism.
_____Fear comes when we think we are responsible for bringing about this protection ourselves.
_____Just believing God in your heart is enough. You don't have to SAY that you do.
_____Fear is the opposite of faith.

# MAKE IT REAL: "I WAS KIDNAPPED!"
## Life Connection Testimony

**Escape from Terror in Mary Johnson's own words:** I had gotten an early start that morning to catch up on my chores. We live 12 miles into the country, so I was surprised to be interrupted by a young man in an old van—supposedly lost—asking for a drink of water. But the pretense was over when he pulled a gun and told me to get in the car. My surprised scream was soon stifled, however, when he threatened my life if I did that again. I was thrown into the back of the van and where a second man wearing a nylon stocking on his head put athletic tape over my mouth and hands and covered my head with a black windbreaker. Black shag carpet covered the sides, floor and roof of the van and the windows were covered with black curtains.

I couldn't tell where they were taking me. I know we crossed railroad tracks and ended up on a gravel road. I had never been so frightened in my life. All I could think about was that I was soon to be 50— soon to be a grandmother—and I wasn't sure I would live to see either; but my greatest fear was being raped. Finally, however, I came to my senses and started claiming my spiritual covenant promise of protection. I suddenly realized—*I was a child of God—fear was of the devil—and I had the protection of God on my life.*

By this time we had stopped and with a wool cap pulled down over my face, I was led over a barbed wire fence and across a pasture to an old, abandoned, ranch house where I was handcuffed to the bathroom lavatory and asked, "What would be the best way to get your husband to cooperate without alerting the police?" Then I was warned if he went to the police he would never see me again—alive! A phone call with all the usual kidnapping threats and instructions was planned, and then I was left to my dilemma.

Still quoting my promises, singing hymns of deliverance and thanking God, I was frantically working to get the pipes loose, but they wouldn't budge. God said in Psalm 91: 15 *"In your day of trouble, call upon Me and I will answer."* I started praying, "Lord, I am calling on You! I can't do this, but You can. Show me a way to get loose." Then for the first time I noticed a tiny pipe coming up the back of the sink. I don't have any idea how I was able to break through, but I know it was a miracle because the FBI agent couldn't believe I was able to do what I did.

Feeling sure the kidnappers would make their call to Don and be back shortly, I was out the back door and over the fence in no time. I had no idea where I was, but I was confident God would get me where I needed to be. Twelve miles later I came to a house with every door locked except the front door. (I later found out the lady never left her doors unlocked, except on this particular day.) After several calls the Sheriff was on his way to get me, but my husband had already left for Goldthwaite, Texas, with the ransom money.

The kidnappers skipped the first meeting but called at 12:30 that night with a new appointed place to meet in Austin, Texas. Obviously, they didn't know I had escaped. This time it was the Texas Rangers who met and took the first man into custody, and later apprehended the second one. I was called to Austin by the FBI to pick him out of a "line-up." All I asked was for the men in the line-up to wear a ball cap and say, "Would you get me a glass of water?" With that, I was able to successfully pick him out of the group and my job was over.

I thank God for His covenant of protection in Psalm 91. We do not have to be afraid of the *"terror of what man can do to us—it will not approach us...."*

**Author's Note:** The man who was convicted of this crime was no amateur criminal. According to police investigation he had a habitual crime problem since his youth and had previously been convicted and imprisoned for robbery, indecency and sexual assault. For this present offense he was sentenced to 99 years in prison. The sheriff told Mrs. Johnson they had never had anyone in their local jail as malicious as this man. The FBI was shocked Mrs. Johnson was able to escape and even more shocked that she had not been beaten, raped or murdered. One of the FBI Agents made this comment, "We cannot believe we are sitting here today with you and you are alive and well."

1.  How did Mary speaking her promise change her situation?

2.  Natural weapons do not work against a spiritual enemy.  According to 2 Corinthians 10: 4-5 why do spiritual weapons work?  Because they are _____ empowered.

3.  When Mary came to her senses she remembered to claim the promises…
    Under pressure have you committed special verses to memory so that your mind would remember to quote God's word and not panic?

*Talk/Write about someone who has experienced a miraculous deliverance from terror in his or her life.*

# MAKE IT MINE:   EVIL COMING FROM ALL DIRECTIONS

Life Relevance Project

# Use the Internet or cut out newspaper headlines that cover the
# four types of horrors.

*For Example:*

Terror by night: **Fugitive Arrested After Allegedly Stealing Purse**

A 24-year-old man wanted in four states on suspicion of assault, auto theft, and burglary was arrested Monday after allegedly stealing a woman's purse as she entered a grocery store on Maple Street.

Arrow that flies by day: **U.S. soldiers die in Afghan battle**

KABUL, Afghanistan (AP) -- Militants armed with rocket-propelled grenades attacked U.S. troops patrolling in the remote northeast of Afghanistan, killing three soldiers before American forces repelled the assault with artillery fire, an official said Saturday.

Pestilence that stalks in darkness: **Teen Battles State over Cancer Treatment**

(Court TV) -- In Virginia, age 16 is old enough to drive a car, work a 40-hour week, stand trial in adult court, and marry.  Starchild Abraham Cherrix, 16, has refused chemotherapy and wants to use an herbal treatment…

Destruction that lays waste at noon: **Quake rocks Mexico City**

MEXICO,  A moderate earthquake rocked Mexico City on Friday, causing skyscrapers to sway and frightening residents, but emergency officials said no major damage or injuries were reported.

# *Consider Publishing Your Story in the Newspaper!*

*Author's Note: While we were in Bacolod City in the Philippines we found out about this remarkable testimony that had taken place right there where we were ministering. During a Psalm 91 discussion, I issued the challenge that seldom does one hear of someone who has a gun pointed at them using the power in the Name of Jesus. Afterwards, a woman in the conference said to my daughter, "Your mother needs to meet Alma Reyes!" It took awhile to trace Alma to her new address in Australia to do this interview and get pictures, but this is her story... [Alma gave an interview to the newspaper "The Asia Christian" in Makati, Philippines]*

On one particular day, less than a year after Alma had accepted Jesus as her Lord and Savior, she got a chance to prove the faithfulness of her God. Bacolod is a large city, bustling with activity while jeepney mini-buses and bicycle carts carry people to their destinations. As usual, Alma was in a commercial jeepney on her way to work. It was routine for the open-air van to stop many times along the way, picking up other passengers until the driver had a full load, but this particular morning Alma had such an uneasiness that she began to pray silently. When the van reached a more secluded area, two men suddenly commanded the driver to stop, stepped off the van, drew out a gun and pointed it to the man sitting next to Alma. Perhaps, it was the scripture, "I will not die but live and proclaim what the Lord has done for me," that God had given to Alma just a month after she got saved that gave her so much confidence that she felt no fear. But when the gunman fired his gun, hitting the man sitting next to Alma in the shoulder, she was the only one on the van who didn't begin screaming hysterically. The panic was so great that an old Chinese man began having a heart attack just as the gunman put his gun to the already wounded man's head, shot and killed him instantly. That was too much. Instead of cringing in fear, a confident boldness in God's protection rose up on the inside of Alma and she turned to look straight into the eyes of the killer, making him so intimidated that he turned his gun to point it directly between Alma's eyes. But before he was able to pull the trigger, she was taking her authority in the Name of Jesus, commanding Satan, in Jesus' Name, to loose His hold on the man. It was obvious that the man was trying to pull the trigger, but his hand was paralyzed and he couldn't move his finger. He tried three times to shoot Alma, to no avail. The driver took off, leaving the killer standing in the road with his gun raised and still trying to shoot it, but it was not until they were out of the killer's range that they heard his gun fire.

By this time everyone's attention was directed toward the old man who was having the heart attack. Alma called to the driver to take the man to the hospital, but as they were going she took his hand and began praying. At that moment the power of God surged through her and he was instantly healed. The old man was so well that by the time they reached the hospital he wouldn't let them take him in because he said that there was no need since he was completely well.

Psalm 91 speaks of the authority that we have been given over the powers of darkness if we decide to use it. Alma is a living testimony to that truth.

# Bible Interaction

(List other Scriptures which relate to this chapter six) Hebrews 8:6; Exodus 12: 23; 2 Corinthians 5:7; I Samuel 17; Romans 10: 9-10; Mark 16: 17-18; I Timothy 4: 1-5; Exodus 23:25

**Link to Last Week:** God shields you from harm and covers you.

**Bait to Next Week:** You do not have to be afraid of the attacks of the enemy that are sent to wound you.

## *Respond With Your Heart*

*What terrors by night currently have an influence in my life?* _____

_____

*In what ways can I overcome these fears?* _____

_____
_____
_____
_____

*How am I choosing to respond to fear when it surfaces?* _____

_____
_____

*What things have I chosen over God in the past when fear surfaced?*

_____
_____

# LESSON SIX: I WILL NOT FEAR THE ARROW
## READ CHAPTER SEVEN      THEME: THE SECOND CATEGORY OF EVIL

Read Psalm 91:5b: "You will not be afraid of... the arrow that flies by day..."

## Points to Ponder

Read the story below or choose a volunteer to read the story aloud to the group. Answer the following questions.

Staff Sergeant Heath Adams had gone hunting with Jeff, one of his Air Force buddies. Upon seeing a coyote, Jeff traded places with Heath and jumped in the passenger seat of the pickup for a better view. Since the bi-pod on his rifle was longer than the gun barrel, he couldn't put the barrel down so he rested the 30-06 rifle between his legs, facing up. Somehow the jostling of the pickup caused the gun to fire, sending a 180 grain bullet through his chest and arm pit. Jeff started screaming he had been hit and to Heath's dismay, he saw a bloody mass of muscle and tissue. The concussion from the blast alone was so strong it blew out the back window. In an instant Heath pulled off his jacket, put it under Jeff's arm and then applied pressure to the arm and chest wound in an effort to stop the bleeding. Simultaneously, he was holding pressure against Jeff's arm, gripping the steering wheel to hold it steady as he drove rapidly on the icy road, and searching for service with his cell phone. He did it all without mishap which was nothing short of a miracle.

Heath was able to get through with his cell phone to the 911 dispatcher, but he still had to drive the 22 mile stretch to the nearest town. That, too, may have been part of God's plan because it gave him time to declare God's promise from Psalm 91. Heath said later that he was not about to let Jeff die because Jeff was not *born again** and he was determined no flaming arrow of the enemy was going to take his buddy out before he made Jesus the Lord of his life. The whole ordeal was miraculous as Jeff underwent six hours of surgery and came out with no permanent damage.

1. Do you think this story would have had the same ending if Jeff had been out hunting with one of his secular friends?

2. What did Heath do that literally saved Jeff's life?

3. Discuss the importance of having friends who know how to believe God's Word.

* Heath led Jeff to the Lord a year later.

# MAKE IT MEANINGFUL:
## Life Application Questions

1. Write out Psalm 91:5b_____

_____

2. What is the second category of evil covered by this text?

3. Write the definition of an arrow used in this context: _____

_____

4. What does this category include?

5. Where are these arrows aimed?

6. In what area does the enemy attack us?

7. What does Ephesians 6:12 tell us?

8. When arrows are sent to wound us, what does God want us to do?

9. We have a _____ with God, telling us _____

_____.

## MAKE IT REAL: INTERNAL ARROWS
### Life Connection Parable

Larry had struggled with his hot temper all of his life. He remembered losing a little league game for all of his team mates because he couldn't control his temper when the umpire called him "out." He had gotten so out of control that the umpire disqualified the team. There were many more similar incidents in his lifetime. The next occasion that caused him extreme embarrassment was an event that took place in front of a girl he was really fond of. He had so lost his cool that all he remembered was seeing the love of his young life pick up her things and literally walk out on him. Even that heartbreak was not enough, however, to bring lasting change in his behavior.

A teaching on Psalm 91 came at a time when Larry was at an all time low. When he heard that he did not have to be afraid of the arrow (the assignment of the enemy), it dawned on him that these outbursts of anger were coming from an assignment from the enemy to destroy his life. The fact that he didn't have to fear losing control any longer ignited faith in his heart and he began thanking God for this portion of his covenant that gave him victory over an internal enemy assignment like anger. Today Larry is a new man. Opportunities to blow up still present themselves, but he is quick to remind the devil that is a part of his old nature—*all things have become new.*

1. Psalm 91 is not automatic. What did Larry have to do to appropriate his covenant?

2. Did knowing this covenant eliminate the temptation to lose his temper?

3. Name some other assignments (arrows), other than anger that might fall under this category.

FEARLESSNESS — "you will not be afraid of...the arrows" sent by the enemy.
Arrows are intentional. They are placed in a bow and aimed. They are meant to harm.
The Fear of bad things happening to us has to be dealt with because fear opens DOORS!

<u>Arrows</u> that Fly by *Day*: **Enemy Assignments** sent to wound you—
an area of Rebellion, Fear, Offense...

***Talk/Write about someone who has experienced a miracle deliverance from an arrow that flies by day.***

## MAKE IT MINE: NATURAL SHIELDS AND SUPERNATURAL SHIELDS
### LIFE RELEVANCE PROJECT

**You wouldn't leave your house without being naturally dressed, so why leave without being spiritually dressed, as well?**

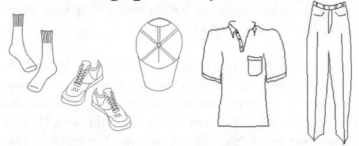

**Ephesians 6:13 tells us to put on the full armor of God so we can withstand all the evil of the day. Don't try to fight the battle alone and in the natural; God has already provided all the weapons we need!**

**Various occupations need protective gear.**

**Name 5 different types of natural protection gear that man uses:**

_____
_____
_____
_____
_____

**Ephesians 6: 12-17 names the elements in the armor of God.**
**Without looking, list the armor and the corresponding virtue it represents:**

**Name of GEAR:**                    **Name of VIRTUE:**

_____            _____
_____            _____
_____            _____
_____            _____
_____            _____

# Bible Interaction

(List other Scriptures which relate to this chapter.)
Ephesians 6: 16

---

**Bonus Study:  FEAR draws like a MAGNET**

Fear is not a "nice" sin but has to be dealt with severely to get it out of our lives. Do a special study on these verses about fear which shows how fear works like a magnet to draw evil toward us...

**Proverb 10:24** "The fear of the wicked shall come upon them..."
**Job 3:25**  "For the thing which I greatly feared is come upon me,
            and that which I was afraid of is come unto to me..."
**Isaiah 54:14**  "You will be far from oppression, for thou shalt not fear;
            and from terror, for it shall not come near thee."
The converse of this verse implies that fear draws oppression to us... but by staying out of fear—oppression and terror cannot come near.

---

## Link to Last Week: **Pray out loud:** "Thank you, Father, that I will not be afraid of what another person can do to harm me. I am in covenant with you."

## Bait to Next Week: My covenant also covers my physical health.

## *Respond With Your Heart*

*Toward what area in my life is the enemy aiming arrows?* _____
_____
_____

*How am I overcoming these arrows?* _____
_____
_____

*How am I trusting God to deliver me from these arrows?* _____
_____
_____

# LESSON SEVEN: I WILL NOT FEAR THE PESTILENCE
## READ CHAPTER EIGHT    THEME: THE THIRD CATEGORY OF EVIL

Reflect on Psalm 91:6a: "You will not be afraid of the pestilence that stalks in darkness."

### Points to Ponder

Read the anecdote below or choose a volunteer to read the story aloud to the group. Answer the following questions.

My good friends, Vicki and Gerald, told me that one of their fellow church members, Dane, developed a small growth in his ear in January of 2006. The doctor decided to remove it in day surgery; however, the "minor" surgery turned out not to be so minor. A biopsy revealed the growth to be *squamous carcinomas*, a very dangerous and aggressive form of skin cancer. He was told to go immediately to an oncologist. Vicki began spending two to three hours every day encouraging Dane and his wife, Diana, with God's covenant promise in Psalm 91. The prognosis from the oncologist/surgeon was grim and frightening. Dane was then sent for a PET scan that showed the cancer had metastasized into the bones in front of and behind his ear. It had also spread to the lymph nodes on the left side of his neck. Surgery was immediately scheduled and two CAT scans were done the day before the surgery. Vicki said that she had never interceded so much for one person before Dane. The Lord even woke her in the middle of the night to pray, and He gave her a vision of how He was going to use Dane to touch his church and usher in a fresh outpouring of the Holy Spirit.

On the day of the surgery Vicki and Diana were permitted to go into a restricted area to pray for Dane, and as they prayed everything came to a complete stop. Even the doctors joined them in prayer. Then three hours later one of the doctors came out to share THE GOOD NEWS! They had begun the surgery by removing the cancerous growth along with surrounding tissue. The tissue was sent to pathology to make sure they had reached the outer parameters of the unhealthy cells. They also made an incision down the left side of Dane's neck to prepare to remove the lymph nodes along with "all other glands" to insure the disease would be contained.

Can you imagine the surprise of the doctors when the report came back from pathology that the test showed the very dangerous and aggressive skin cancer wasn't *squamous* at all, but *basal cell carcinomas*—which very rarely spread to any other parts of the body! The doctors closed Dane's neck and did not remove the lymph nodes.

In addition, the doctor told them the CAT scans that had been done the day before had shown a completely different story from the PET scan the week prior. The first CAT scan indicated there was no cancer in the nodes, so the second scan was done—this one indicating there was no cancer in the nodes or bone! The disease was retreating before their very eyes, and by the time they did the surgery, the threat of death had been rebuked by the Lord.

The doctor was confused and kept saying, "I don't know how this happened!" It was all that Vicki and Diana could do to keep from just running through the hospital, praising God. Dane was supposed to be in the hospital for several days and then have chemo and radiation treatment, but he went home the day after surgery, cancer free. Thank God, *the things which are seen are temporal and subject to change...,*" according to 2 Corinthians 4: 18.

1. How is this story a testimony of why we should walk by faith and not by sight?


2. Why is it important to stand on God's Word, despite negative reports?


3. How could this story have ended differently if Vicki, Gerald, Dane and Diana hadn't let God's Word be the final authority?


# MAKE IT MEANINGFUL:
### Life Application Questions

1. Write out Psalm 91:6a:

_____

_____

2. What is the third category of evil covered by this text?


3. Write the definition of Pestilence (Chapter 3/Lesson 3) : _____

_____


4. How did God get our attention with this promise?


5. What does it include?


6. Faith is not a _____.


7. Faith is simply the _____ to _____ what He says in His Word.

8. What does Mark 13:31 say?


9. How can our inheritance be what Jesus provided for us?

10. The curses are listed in Deuteronomy 28; and Deuteronomy 28: 61 tells us that every sickness, even the ones not listed, are all part of the curse!   What does Galatians 3:13 say?

11. True or false?
_____God cannot protect me if I drink or inhale something poisonous!

12. What does Mark 16:17-18 say? (Military)

13. No _____ has been _____ by man, against which _____ has not provided a _____ _____ of _____ for any of _____ who will _____ to _____ _____ and _____. (Military)

14. When we bless our food before eating what are we doing? (Military)

15. What are we told to do in I Timothy 4:1-5 and Exodus 23:25? (Military)

16. This is not for everyone; it is for those _____. (Military)

17. Does pestilence mean biblical diseases only?

18.  Did the author expand the meaning of pestilence for you in this chapter, and if so how?

19. What we allow our _____ to dwell on is our _____.

20. How do we operate in this protective covenant?

# MAKE IT REAL: SICKNESS AND THE POWER OF GOD'S WORD
Life Connection Parable

Renea was a teenager who had grown up in a church who did lip-service to believing in the doctrine of healing and protection but personally, she had never heard a real-life testimony of a miracle. Healing was never taught as a possibility for modern people, but Renea's interest in the subject was aroused each time a passage about it came up in the church sermons. While reading through her Bible, she noticed that Jesus seemed to have fun when he healed the sick and even asked a couple of times which is easier: healing or forgiveness? Then He would do both. Renea was struck by the variety of ways in which Jesus healed the sick and how He did not have a mechanical way of dealing with sickness.

When Renea was diagnosed with a brain tumor, she did not fall to pieces like the rest of her family who were devastated by the news. No one could fathom any spiritual side to healing, only the increasingly dire predictions that she had been diagnosed as a fatal case.

Renea had to fight for her life, but she was up to the challenge. She explored different ways she could be healed based on what she saw in the Scripture. She knew she could be anointed with oil; she saw a precedence for Jesus just speaking the word; she saw the disciples laying on hands; she read of the woman touching the hem of Jesus' garment and being healed.

Renea wrote down lists of creative ideas for receiving her healing. She watched a movie about the life of Christ and when she saw the part where Jesus was brutally beaten by a Roman whip, the scripture in Isaiah 53: 5 went deep into her heart: "Jesus bore those stripes so I, Renea, am healed." She rewound and watched that scene over and over releasing her faith that *Jesus is the same yesterday, today and forever (Hebrews 13:8)*. Watching Jesus take that punishment, healing became a personal reality to Renea. She came to the conclusion that her point of contact was letting her little brother lay hands on her and pray, since a child tends to have unwavering faith. Renea has been nick-named the "miracle child" by her family and doctors. She now is a grown woman beginning a family of her own, completely free of the tumor with no side effects--all because she believed that receiving Jesus' payment for our healing is no more difficult than our receiving Jesus' payment for our sins.

1. What ultimately led to Renea's healing?

2. Why was it easy for Renea not to overreact or give up when she received her diagnosis?

3. What was the importance of having her little brother pray for her when there were many people who were much older and more mature?

4. Why can we believe for healing as easily as for our sins being erased?

**REMINDER:** <u>FEARLESSNESS</u> — "you will not be afraid of…"
  The fear of pestilence must be dealt with.  Pay special attention to the verb "stalks".

Fear opens DOORS to <u>Pestilence</u> that Stalks in *Darkness*:
  **Fatal Diseases and Epidemics** (Take note that God repeats pestilence twice in this Psalm.)

He doesn't promise a world free from PESTILENCE…but PROTECTION in it!
  *This is a risky world.*

### *Talk/Write about someone who has experienced a miracle of healing in his or her life.*

This is a **SPECIFIC PROJECT** for those struggling in the particular area of a long sickness or persistent malady which refuses to let up:

## MAKE IT MINE:          GET OUT OF THE RUT!

### *When an illness or problem refuses to budge, what do you do?*
*Sometimes we get in the rut of trying to resist every thing in the same old way. The Bible has much variety in its methods.  The same with testimonies…*
When you listen to a person tell of a  healing you hear testimonies from every point of the spectrum — people partaking of the Lord's supper as a point of contact to a child praying in faith over an ill adult.

*Role-play:*
  *Choose two people to re-enact the different ways Jesus healed people:  For example: He spoke to the infirmity, told the person something specific to do, put His fingers in their ears and commanded them to open, etc.*

  *Choose two people to re-enact how people were healed by the early church in the book of Acts.*

  *Choose two people to re-enact the healings by Elijah and Elisha in the Old Testament.*
    *Go through the passages acting out how the miracle was performed…*

Many times God will speak to you at the hearing of His Word. I have experienced healing in a variety of ways. Once I was attending an Easter reenactment of Christ's life at a small Baptist church in a neighboring town and was in much pain. When the Jesus "actor" passed by my seat, to my complete surprise, I suddenly was instantly free from pain that I had for weeks. God will give us different ways and specific instructions on how to release our faith in this area.

# MAKE IT MINE:       THE EXCHANGE SYSTEM
### Life Relevance Project

Make a chart of types of fear the devil throws at us in an attempt to plague us with pestilence or fear.

List a short prayer or promise to counteract that attack.

| Pestilence or Fear: | Prayer or Promise |
|---|---|
| The devil sends fear of disease or sickness | Matthew 8:17 says that Jesus died on the cross for our sickness. |
| The devil sends fear of failure | Philippians 4:13 says, "I can do all things through Christ which strengthens me." |
| The devil sends depression | Nehemiah 8:10 says, "The joy of the Lord is my strength." |
| The devil sends thoughts of chaos | 1 Cor. 2:16 says, "I have the mind of Christ." |

## List your own examples:

| | |
|---|---|
| | |
| | |
| | |
| | |

**Bible Interaction**
(List other Scriptures which relate to this chapter)
Matthew 8: 17, Isaiah 53: 5, 2 Corinthians 4: 18, Galatians 3: 13, Deuteronomy 28,
I Timothy 4:1-5, Exodus 23:25, Mark 16: 17-18, Luke 21: 11; Mark 13: 31

**Link to Last Week:** I no longer have to put up with the enemy assignments that have plagued me and hindered my walk with the Lord.

**Bait to Next Week:** Is there any kind of personal protection provided for relating to natural disasters? Next week we will look at this fourth category of evil.

## *Respond With Your Heart*

*What pestilences are stalking my life?* _____

_____

_____

_____

*How am I overcoming the enemy in that area?* _____

_____

_____

_____

*How often do I take authority over negative thoughts and emotions?*

_____

_____

_____

_____

# Journal

# Lesson Eight: I Will Not Fear the Destruction
## Read Chapter Nine          Theme: The Fourth Category of Evil

**Read Psalm 91:6b:** "You will not be afraid of the destruction that lays waste at noon."

### Points to Ponder

Read the anecdote below or choose a volunteer to read the story aloud to the group. Answer the following questions.

For Peggy Joyce's son, Bill, life at college had been eventful to say the least. He and a roommate had asked a couple of girls from the Christian university he was attending for a dinner date at a local Mexican restaurant. Not knowing the girls were as big of pranksters as himself, he was in shock when they came down to join the guys, fully dressed in wedding gowns with bouquets. Sure enough, when they got to the car, it had been targeted, as well, with *Just Married* painted on the windows in shoe polish and a string of tin cans tied to the rear bumper. Bill, the dorm-wing prankster, had been out-pranked. The sheer boldness of these two girls and the awkwardness of being caught off guard on a first date soon turned into a night with even another twist. The roommate's car broke down in the middle of the road and a tow truck had to come to pull them to safety and fix their car. When Bill, who was trying to survive on a college student's allowance, pulled out cash to pay the guy, the man took one look at the car and at the two girls and said, "We couldn't charge you guys on a night like this!" For the moment Bill had forgotten what the girls had done and followed the burly mechanic's nod toward the two girls huddled in wedding dresses in the car. Bill was speechless and was still trying to think of how to explain the situation as the guy drove away, but later thanked his date for inadvertently saving him a pile of money for a repair job which normally would have ruined a first date. Some things come toward our life bearing no real danger, yet at other times something we are not spiritually prepared for can destroy us, like what hit Bill unexpectedly the very next week…

Bill was driving eight hours home in his truck with three passengers in the cab—all girls: his sister, Angie, her roommate and the girl who the week before had given him the shock of dressing in a wedding dress on the first date. Since her hometown was near Bill's, he offered her a ride home to save her money on gasoline. Conversation was light and lively as the hilarious "wedding dress prank/double date event" was recounted in detail in the truck cab, when suddenly, Bill yelled. An eighteen wheeler truck was coming down the one-way service road straight at them. They only had time for one word as they braced for the collision. "Jesus!" they screamed as Bill braked furiously, in vain. There wasn't even time for a formal prayer, just a unified one word plea for help. The truck driver's face was in terror as he realized he was hitting a truck full of youth head-on, whose faces he could see. The four in the truck closed their eyes as the two vehicles were ready to slam together. Everyone wishes that they had kept their eyes open because when they opened them…there was no truck in front of them.

The truck was stopped behind them and the driver looked bewildered. No one knows, for sure, what happened after that split second prayer. *Did the angels carry them under the truck? Did the truck go over them?* Everyone had closed their eyes for the impact. All they know is that when they called on the name of the Lord, God delivered them in an instant from total destruction.

It is amazing how instantaneously a happy situation can turn into a nightmare—a "wedding" could have turned into a funeral. Danger can come out of nowhere to destroy our lives. It is so important to realize the power of what this passage in Psalm 91 tells us about the four categories of evil and what God says about our protection.

1. Compare the difference between the two "unexpected" events in this story.

2. How could this situation have ended differently, if it hadn't been for God's protection?

3. How did the covenant of this psalm protect the vehicles without even a formal prayer?

4. Is there a way to pray Psalm 91 preventatively before you face an unexpected or sudden danger?

 ## MAKE IT MEANINGFUL:
### Life Application Questions

1. Write out Psalm 91:6b _____

_____

2. What is the first category of evil covered by this text?_____

_____

3. Write the definition of "destruction": _____

_____

4. What does destruction include?_____

_____

5. God says not to be afraid of any of those things because_____

_____

6. What did Jesus do in Mark 4:39?_____

_____

7. What does this demonstrate?_____

8. What does God want us to do when we are threatened with destruction?_____

_____

9. What has God offered us regarding every extreme evil known to man? _____

_____

10. What is the one condition for protection from all four categories of evil?_____

_____

11. What is the secret to receiving anything that God has already provided?_____

_____

12. God offered this _____ to us before we even had a chance to _____!

13. If you can _____ where God has offered it, you can _____ it. His provision is

_____ _____ - waiting to be _____.

14. When God created us, He automatically made Himself _____ to _____ for us and

_____. (Military)

15. If faith is not a _____ with which to _____ God, what is it?

16. God does not make _____ that are _____ of our _____.

17. What does it say in Romans 3:3-4?_____

_____

18. What is a very important part, a reminder from the Old Testament, of that verse?_____

_____

# MAKE IT REAL: DESTRUCTION OUT THE FRONT DOOR!
Life Connection Parable

A year after Hurricane Ivan hit, we stayed in the beach home at Orange Beach, Alabama of our friends, John and Virginia. For one week we just drove through the area, appalled at the devastation we saw—even after months of repairs had taken place. A stone's throw from their house—all the decking at the public boat docks, the gigantic dry dock building, and the restaurant glass had all been blown away. What was left of the marina building had had three feet of water standing in it. And then on the other side of the house, we saw pictures of the shopping center where there was nothing left but a pile of rubble. Condos and hotels were completely gutted. Even after that length of time there were mounds of siding and roofing shingles from the homes next to their beach home still littering the adjacent properties.

Only after seeing the destruction with our own eyes did we realize the supernatural protection our friends had received. Prior to and during the hurricane the year before, they had called us several times, stating their total trust in the Lord's Psalm 91 covenant promise of protection and getting us to join in faith with them. **When they returned to the area there was NO damage to their beach house or property.** When a hurricane passes over, flooding brings much of the destruction because the water goes everywhere. Only God knows how He kept the water out of their beach home! **THE WORD WORKS!** And did I forget to mention that, at the time, they also owned a beach front condo just three blocks away that was on the market for sale. The condo was directly on the beach, but when John opened the door to the condo not even a picture on the wall had been disturbed, nor was the patio glass door broken. Yet the eye of Hurricane Ivan had gone directly over the top of their building. Coincidence? If you had driven down Beach Road (even a year later, when we did) you would know it was nothing but the power of God's protection that protected them. Praise God! Psalm 91 is not limited to areas where hurricanes can't reach. We can even be immune in the midst of mass destruction.

1.  How can you appropriate Psalm 91's promises for protection of your property?

2.  Destruction comes to wreak havoc with our life. Do you have a story which is similar to this where God protected your home or property?

**REMINDER:** FEARLESSNESS — "you will not be afraid of…destruction (natural disasters)"
Fear has to be dealt with because fear opens DOORS to the
"Destruction that lays Waste at Noon": Tornadoes, Hurricanes, Earthquakes, Car Wrecks.
He doesn't promise a world FREE FROM DESTRUCTION…but PROTECTION in it!

*Talk/Write about someone who has experienced a miraculous deliverance from natural disasters.*

# MAKE IT MINE: PRAYER PETITIONS
### Life Relevance Project

## PRAYING FOR OTHERS.....

Start a network of people you can pray for specifically in your secret prayer closet for particular needs they have and for their protection. Keep a prayer journal of specific answers that God gives you and date the requests. Do not forget to pray for those who are in high places of authority over your life, as well as those who are going through crisis.

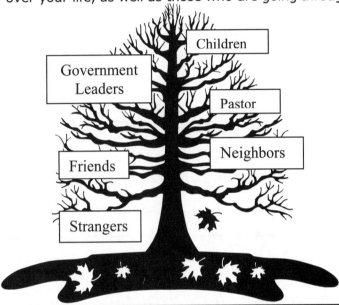

When Washington was consumed with fear, one man prayed. Sniper shootings had paralyzed a city. People were afraid to stop to get gas, they would not let their children out of the home in the DC, Maryland and Virginia communities. Random sniper bullets had killed 10 and wounded 3 more, and there is no telling how many more victims there would have been if this one man had not decided to pray.

**Ron Lantz** decided to do something about the terror that the whole region was in—he would organize a prayer meeting. This was not your regular prayer meeting. He was a trucker rolling down the interstate, listening to talk radio, when he used his CB to call anyone listening to pray. Fifty Christian truckers got together to pray that somehow the ones responsible would be caught. Then Ron had another impression in his spirit. He told the other truckers that God was going to use him to catch the sniper. Fifty truck drivers had decided to do something about the problem, and they prayed for about 58 minutes in this impromptu prayer meeting.

A few days later Ron was listening to the radio as he was again driving through the same area and felt **compelled** to pull off the highway at a rest stop. It was just a couple of miles from where he had arranged the prayer meeting. As he pulled in, lo, and behold, right before his eyes was the Chevrolet Caprice that was described on the radio. He had found what none of the best law enforcement agents and special teams could find.

A tingle went up his spine when the license plate matched what he had scribbled down and he quickly called 911. He wasn't afraid, but said the fifteen minute wait for the police was the longest of his life. Then, not fearing for his own safety, he pulled his truck rig in a position to block the snipers. There is no way of knowing how many more innocent victims were saved that day.

When Ron had first heard the bad news reports, he believed the word of God enough, that, instead of acting in fear, he acted in faith.

Adapted from Charisma Magazine, Feb 2003, Robert Anderescik.

# Bible Interaction

(List other Scriptures which relate to this chapter)
Mark 4:39, Romans 3:3-4

**Link to Last Week:** I can walk free from pestilence.

**Bait to Next Week:** It is horrible to see a day which actually has thousands falling by our side. Some days it feels as though we are the only ones standing. Next week let's find out how we don't have to be one of the 10,000 who fall.

## *Respond With Your Heart*

*What types of destruction are plaguing my life right now?*

_____

_____

_____

*In what ways am I overcoming the destruction?* _____

_____

_____

_____

*What area of my life needs to be renewed by the Word of God?*

_____

_____

_____

*What promises am I claiming against enemy attacks?* _____

_____

_____

# LESSON NINE: THOUSANDS FALLING...
## READ CHAPTER TEN   THEME: HORRORS WILL BE ON ALL SIDES OF YOU

**STUDY**: Psalm 91:7-9: "A thousand may fall at your side and ten thousand at your right hand; but it shall not approach you. You will only look on with your eyes, and see the recompense of the wicked. For you have made the Lord, my refuge even the Most High, your dwelling place..."

### Points to Ponder

**Read the anecdote below or choose a volunteer to read the story aloud to the group. Answer the following questions.**

In the introduction of *Psalm 91: Military Edition,* a story is told of how this psalm literally saved a lieutenant's life. He committed himself to the Lord, but was immediately shot in the chest. When a buddy saw him go down, he grabbed his carbine out of his hands and began blasting away with a gun in both hands. Not one enemy was left standing. Later, the lieutenant's sister in Pennsylvania received a letter telling the story: The blast to the chest knocked him to the ground. He felt the impact and reached for the wound, but instead he felt his Bible in his pocket. He stared at the ugly hole in the Bible. That Bible had been in his pocket directly over his heart and he looked to where the bullet had gone. As the lieutenant thumbed through the pages, the bullet had passed through Genesis, Exodus, Leviticus, Numbers, and had gone through book after book, stopping in the middle of the Ninety-first Psalm, pointing like a finger to verse 7—*A thousand will fall at your side and ten thousand by your right hand, but it will not come near you.* The lieutenant was not even aware of that verse until that moment, but God had supernaturally revealed it to him. Psalm 91 is literal. Psalm 91 is reliable. Your protection may not be as dramatic as it was with this army lieutenant, but your promises are just as real. What God promises you in Psalm 91 can LITERALLY save your life!

1. Why did his buddy assume he was dead?




2. Just so no one would think that the bullet was stopped by accident, God marked the verse that applied to his situation. *Was the lieutenant aware of this verse before this incident? Are you familiar with this verse?*




3. How did this soldier's story encourage you to take Psalm 91 literally?

# MAKE IT MEANINGFUL:
### Life Application Questions

1. Write out Psalm 91: 7, 9:  "A _____ may fall at your side and _____ _____ at your right hand; but it shall not _____ you. You will only _____ on with your _____, and see the _____ of the wicked. For you have made the Lord, my _____ even the Most High, your _____ place."

2. What question does the author ask regarding Christians and this verse?

3. Jesus made the same point about unclaimed promises in Luke 4:27, what was it?

4. Who was the only leper cleansed in this passage, and why?

5. Only those who _____ God and hold fast to His _____ will _____.

6. Psalm 91:7 is an awesome statement; what does the author want us to know?

7. The author compares the feeling of fear to which event in the New Testament?

8. The author points out that God is preparing us for fearful times, how, why?

9. What happens now that we have been warned?

10. These are not words for _____ *in* affliction, but words of _____ *from* affliction.

11. Psalm 91 is the _____ measure that God has given to His _____ against _____ _____ known to mankind.

12. Psalm 91 is a _____ and _____ measure to ward off every evil _____ it has time to strike. This is not only a _____, but a plan for _____ _____. (military)

**"The Recompense of the Wicked" Section [Military book, chapter 10]:**

13. Read Matthew 5:18.  "Not the _____ letter or _____ of His Word will _____ away until it is all _____."

14. What does the author point out about truth?

15. When we are in _____ to a degree, we are placing ourselves in the category of the _____. We can be an _____-*believing* believer!

**Bonus:** *Excerpt from Psalm 91: God's Shield.

"Recompense of the Wicked: Does the Wicked Have to Pay?"

Sometimes you will witness *recompense* being doled out. There is judgment. Every sin will be exposed sooner or later. An evil dictator falls, an unrighteous aggressor is stopped. A tyrant faces his crimes against humanity. A wrong is rectified. *The recompense of the wicked speaks of justice.* Wars have been fought to stop aggression and those with a righteous cause ultimately prevail. The justice of God is that evil will not triumph—that "Hitlers" do not win—that communistic governments fall—that darkness does not extinguish light and that, in due course, good does triumph over evil.

This verse says that we will *only look on and see* it happening. The word *only* denotes a protection of only *seeing* and not experiencing the evil, and it denotes detachment in that the evil we see does not get inside of us. We are set apart in that we do not allow our enemy's hate to change us.

Can you think of a war fought where one side had a righteous cause?

Name a way in which we can become like our enemy? _____ .
The Bible promises that good will win in the end and recompense will be distributed.

Do we have our personal sins recompensed/paid for?

16. How does Psalm 91:8 say we deal with disaster?

17. Many people think of the Gospel as an _____ _____, securing only their _____ and their _____ after _____ strikes.

18. God's Word is more than just an _____ from Hell; it is a _____ for living a _____ life in this world.

19. What does II Timothy 3:12 tell us?

20. There are times when we will be _____ because of our stand for the cause of Christ, but what are we never to put up with?

***Talk/Write about an experience where you allowed God's Word to be your final authority above an experience, circumstance or emotion.***

# MAKE IT REAL: ONLY LOOK ON WITH YOUR EYES
## Life Connection Parable

Kyle just couldn't believe what he was reading in Psalm 91. It seemed too good to be true and it was almost ridiculous to think that these verses had any literal meaning above mere comfort to its readers. Kyle had heard a testimony shared on the radio and he could not forget the strength of the words: *a thousand will fall at your side and ten thousand will fall by your right hand but it will not approach you. You will only look on with your eyes…*

Kyle called the station to ask which passage the verse was taken from. Now he was reading the verse in context. How could he believe such a thing? God clearly didn't give Himself any "outs" or loopholes in the promises He was making. Kyle was from a Christian family that was riddled with bad fortune. He had watched a brother waste away from a painful disease in early childhood. His grandmother was a good woman who had died in an automobile wreck. They didn't come any better than this unselfish woman who was the Christian matriarch of the family. Yet, what really caught Kyle's attention was the part of the verse that talked about seeing disaster all around you—his job was running from one emergency scene to another. He was a first responder that worked with the EMS unit and he had seen every conceivable type of death and disaster. His emotions had become numb through the years from the adrenaline rush, the nauseating smell of death and accidents. What bothered him most were the children.

Was this passage for him? Experience told him that this wasn't a possibility for him. In fact, Kyle had been doing some soul-searching, and he was questioning whether God even cared. That is when he found that the disciples had asked the same question when they were caught in a storm (Mark 4: 38-40) and Jesus seemed angry with them that they doubted His compassion or whether He cared for them. Similarly, Kyle knew that God was good from his study of the Bible. Kyle knew mentally that God was love from reading the verse. But his intellect could not talk the emotional pain away.

His accountability partner whose name was David taught him a valuable lesson. He told him that the Bible is truth while circumstances can change. There can be no "what about so-and-so—it didn't seem to work in *his* life." Our faith has to be centered first in what the Word says rather than our past experiences. David said he had encountered a similar crossroads in his life and had decided to take God at His Word no matter what his eyes saw. David declared, "It was like something settled in me when I decided to believe the Word." He said, "Sometimes what we don't understand tries to undo and redefine what we do understand. If we know that God is a good God and doesn't play tricks on us (Matthew 7:9-11), then we can know that sometimes we just don't see the whole picture." Kyle grasped the concept and decided to let the Word of God take the steering wheel of his life. He would let the Word of God change the circumstances of his life, but not let circumstances change the Word. Kyle had always felt like he believed, but, perhaps, today was the first day he believed it at a new depth.

1. Give examples how emotional pain can cause *what we don't understand* to negatively change *what we do understand from God's Word*:


2. God's promises are not always automatic for the Christian. Neither are they a reward for being a good person. What must we do to receive the promises?


3. Have you settled the truth of God's Word despite what circumstances might say?

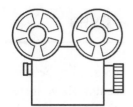

**"The Fallen" [Psalm 91: 7]**  by Angelia Ruth Schum

"What Happens When Psalm 91 Appears Not to Work?"

It is always enjoyable to me to watch mom do **live TV interviews**. There is so much to cover in Psalm 91 that half an hour to an hour just doesn't do this powerful Psalm justice. Yet what about when the interviewer asks the one thing that isn't asked in Psalm 91? Many interviewers skip straight over the strength of the passage, the promises available and the information on how to obtain the protection Psalm 91 offers, and they ask mom the question: *"What happens when Psalm 91 doesn't work?"* For lengthy interviews this is an engaging topic within itself, but this question is something that comes up regularly in short question and answer formats. Mom's quick response was good--*"Honestly it feels like that every single time!"* Mom gave a very pragmatic but truthful answer when she said, *"Usually my mind is screaming: "What if it doesn't work this time?"* I think it is important for us to know that every single time we are facing a test, the enemy asks this question: *What if it doesn't work?* Honestly, it never feels like it is going to work when you are going through it!

We tell the Psalm 91 stories after the knot in our stomach is gone and the raw emotion is over and we have the great testimony. However, when you face it--it looks like failure is coming for you every time. These types of testimonies are only fun on FAST FORWARD! Only after it is over does it make a great testimony. After my eye was healed, after the tornado went back up into the sky, after a loved one comes home from war, after…,after…, after…, etc Mom's candid response was not a flippant answer—she means it when she says there isn't a time you aren't facing that question in the heat of a trial. Yet, I know what the interviewers are alluding to—*"What happens after the fact and it is too late?"* **Mom would encourage you with these thoughts…**

* It would be dangerous to consider any word from God as failing according to Romans 3:3-4. What is interesting about this Psalm--it doesn't address any issue concerning the promises not working. It has no back doors and anything a person would say to answer this in individual cases--would be pure conjecture. It is an odd request to be asked to go further than where the Bible goes. An exegesis on this Psalm is very powerful and in all respects, it dares you to take courage and is written without any apologies.... To be true to the verse by verse text, she stayed with how this Psalm reads.

* Many times people read this psalm to bring them comfort or inspiration. However, Psalm 91 promises deliverance. There is nothing passive about this psalm. If we are hearers only, we can expect the same results as the man who built his house on the sand: a collapse, a failure. Only the man who took the right actions came out of that parable of a storm which Jesus told. As much as we may not like hearing there is something for us to do—Psalm 91 can not be taken passively. <u>Knowing</u> this psalm, <u>living</u> this psalm, <u>saying</u> this psalm and <u>acting</u> on this psalm can be a totally different approach. If you are not aware of the conditional aspects of the psalm or willing to do what it says, you cannot expect the results that it promises.

* <u>However, God does have an answer for those regrets, heartaches and tragic situations which may have already occurred.</u> I'm a big believer in seeing that God's sovereignty is tied up in His ability to work all things for good for those who love Him. There is a certain realm of God, specializing in the impossible, that man can never find on his own. I believe that the worst blow the devil has ever given us, God can turn and use for good, if it is placed in His hands... (Romans 8:28 and Genesis 50:20)

*How would you respond to the question Peggy Joyce is being asked if you were being interviewed?*

# MAKE IT MINE: AROUND THE CLOCK
### Life Relevance Project

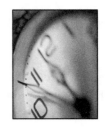

## DAY AND NIGHT
## AROUND THE CLOCK PROTECTION

### MAKE A LIST
### OF THE DIFFERENT TYPES OF DISASTERS PSALM 91 PROTECTS AT THESE TIMES OF DAY:

By Day               _____

By Noon            _____

By Night     (The dead of Night)    _____

In Darkness (Dark hours of Life)    _____

Then make a clock that shows what to pray for at different times of day.

Arrow
that flies
by day

Destruction
that lays waste
at noon

12 1 2 3 4 5 6 7 8 9 10 11

Pestilence
that stalks
in darkness

Terror
by
Night

# Special Excerpt: "Is the "Will Not Approach" verse even Possible?"

**Leslie King's Testimony:** During the entire first year of my deployment to Iraq, there was a very tangible sense of the protective covering of God's Hand. We had not lost a single soldier-- no one in the company had been hurt; in fact, not any one I knew in any personal way had ever been harmed. I felt that same protective covering for everyone I saw. Emotionally, I felt no loss of life impact that usually results from war. I experienced none of the gruesomeness of war during the time I served, even though it was really prevalent in the Iraqi conflict. The prayer covering of the church and my family gave me a totally different battle experience. It wasn't because we hadn't seen danger, because we had. But there was a pervading sense of security over us and everyone that we knew on the battlefield. We had been through "rough stuff" without a scratch and had felt protected and peaceful the whole time! *So dramatic and so tangible was this to me that there were times when I would see one of my buddies in danger and I would go stand in front of him. The protection was so real it was almost as if I could reach out and touch it.*

Probably the strongest promise in Psalm 91 covenant is that it *"will not approach you."*

*#1   What* will not approach us? _____        *What* is falling at our side?_____

#2  Is the *"1000's falling on one side and 10,000 on the other"* referring to:

_____ people falling in a battle scene?

_____ pestilence (fatal diseases) which is attacking the masses?

_____ arrows (falling by a 1000 on one side and 10,000 on the other)

_____ every type of danger mentioned in Psalm 91?

No matter how we define it, this is definitely a scene of combat and a promise of protection at a level not many have experienced.

#3  What can be done to apply this supernatural *"shall not approach you"* kind of protection?

_____

**Leslie King had a spiritual heritage from his hometown.**

**#4 Check similar ones that you have experienced personally:**

____*Seadrift, Texas in WWII prayed as a community Psalm 91 over their soldiers.

____*They would meet daily and read Psalm 91 together.

____*The church put up a billboard of all the men's pictures so they would constantly remember them in prayer.

_____*They paid extra attention to personal nudges the Holy Spirit gave them to intercede:

Excerpt: Grandmother Weaver would get an uptightness in her spirit about the safety of her sons and the men from her town who were fighting in Europe and in the Pacific during WW2, and she would head to the woodshed to intercede. She said she would bombard heaven until she sensed a release in her spirit.

**Leslie King had a spiritual hedge of protection from the prayers of his church.**

**#5  Check similar ones that you experienced personally:**

____* Seadrift remembered what God did in WW2 and prayed again for this generation.

____* Leslie's family kept him covered in prayer.

____* His church put up the soldier's pictures on a billboard so they'd remember to pray.

____* Leslie attended church while he was stationed in Germany and the soldiers committed to pray the psalm for protection.

____ * Leslie believed the words for himself.

This *"shall not approach"* promise is one of the strongest forms of protection named in this psalm.

# Bible Interaction
(List other Scriptures which relate to this chapter)
Luke 4:27, Matthew 5:18, 2 Timothy 3: 12; Romans 5:20b, Psalm 91:8-9

**Link to Last Week:** I am in the world, but not of the world. I do not have to be afraid of the natural disasters happening all around me.

**Bait to Next Week:** We do not have to fear for our families. This next lesson tells us how to appropriate protection for more than just ourselves.

## *Respond With Your Heart*

*Am I taking God's promise in verse seven literally?* _____

_____

_____

_____


*Has the Gospel become more than just an insurance policy in my life?*

_____

_____

_____

_____


*Have I made the Lord my dwelling place according to verse nine?*

_____

_____

_____

_____

# Journal

# LESSON TEN: ANGELIC PROTECTION FOR MY FAMILY
### READ CHAPTERS ELEVEN-TWELVE  THEME: HOUSEHOLD AND PERSONAL PROTECTION

**PSALM 91: 10-12:** "No evil will befall you, nor will plague or calamity come near your dwelling. For He will give His Angels charge concerning you, to guard you in all your ways. They will bear you up in their hands lest you strike your foot against a stone."

## Points to Ponder

Read the anecdote below or choose a volunteer to read the story aloud to the group. Answer the following questions.

When the college team went to Chiapas to provide Christmas for the Mayan children in the villages, my daughter, Angelia, said it was hard to get in the mood for Christmas when it was so hot near the equator. However, the village children were pleased with their toys gathered up by church friends in the states. They never knew it didn't seem right to have Christmas in that kind of heat.

The Mayans volunteered to take the 17 Crosslines college students for a two hour hike up in the mountains to see waterfalls. Justin, a recent college graduate who led the college team, had seen the falls once before. Now he was taking the Americans in to see the jungle with swinging vines, monkeys, exotic birds, and grapefruits that were sweeter than anything anyone had tasted back home.

The Mayan guides could speak no English, but somehow they communicated to us that these were "bad oranges" used only for cooking, and they were very determined that the group not eat them. The two hour journey over several mountains separated the group in many directions; therefore, they were amazed when everyone ended up at the falls several hours later. In the heat the blue water in the pool below the falls was too enticing, so the group plunged in. The Mayan children seemed to get really excited as they watched the Americans swim, and the Mayan guides just stood and observed. The team warned each other that near the falls there was a strong undertow and the water was much too deep to swim against the current. Several of the guys dived in and swam to reach the falls in order to help one of the girls get out of the undertow and on to the rocks. Many of the other team members just leisurely swam around the banks in the refreshing water. We were extremely grateful that no one got lost that day on the hike and that we had been blessed to see and enjoy something so beautiful together.

The next year when Justin and his new bride, Heather, returned as a couple, they went back to that village and to the waterfalls. This time the Mayans were able to communicate something to them that they had not been able to communicate the year before. The Mayan children had been shocked that no one was attacked by alligators. The pool was brimming full of alligators that were two meters long. The villagers knew they would attack any one who fell into the water so it wasn't that the Mayan children couldn't swim—it was that they knew not to go near the water. Instead they had just watched the crazy Americans who didn't know any better!

**MY BROTHER-IN-LAW, LLOYD, MADE THE ANALOGY OF DANIEL IN THE LION'S DEN WHEN HE HEARD ABOUT THE TEAM'S PROTECTION FROM THE ALLIGATORS. HE COULD ENVISION THOSE ALLIGATORS TRYING TO OPEN THEIR MOUTHS TO TAKE A BITE OUT OF THE 17 KIDS IN THE WATER, BUT THE LORD'S ANGELS KEPT THEIR JAWS SHUT TIGHT. IN LIFE, WE ARE OFTEN PROTECTED FROM THINGS THAT WE MAY NEVER KNOW ABOUT UNTIL ETERNITY. EACH OF US HAS STORIES FROM OUR LIVES WHERE WE HAVE BEEN SUPERNATURALLY PROTECTED.**

1. Why is it so important to have established in our heart the Word concerning our protection *before* we need it?

2. Have you ever talked to anyone who has seen an angel?

3. Have you had an experience of supernatural protection where you know some unseen beings kept watch over you?

## MAKE IT MEANINGFUL:
### Life Application Questions

1. Write out Psalm 91:10 - _____
_____

2. What is the *added dimension* to the promise?

3. Why is it important that these promises include our household?

4. Why does it appear that Old Testament leaders had a better understanding of this concept?

5. What does Psalm 112:7 say?
6. What happens as our hearts become truly steadfast in God and we trust His faithfulness to fulfill His promises?

7. _____ _____ will begin to pass away and we will start expecting _____ _____.

8. What should you say when fear knocks on your door? (Military)

9. The beauty of this psalm is that when someone prays for more than himself he _____
_____...? (Military)

## THE POWER OF INTERCESSION

### SPECIAL EXCERPT: Prayer for Son in Military

Edited version of Julie Weise: When my son, Jake, was born, little did I know that 21 years later he would be one of the first United States Marines to cross the border into Iraq. He went into battle with God's Word in his heart. He took his Bible and carried a copy of Psalm 91 in his pocket. We laid hands on him and prayed for his safety.

During those days when we would watch the television and hear reports of the fighting, we took comfort in our faith and in the promises of Psalm 91. Many people were praying and standing with us. There were times when Satan tried to whisper in my ear—thoughts of fear and doubt—thoughts of death and loss. But I have read God's Word and I know His promises. Not just for Heaven, as wonderful as that will be, but also promises of protection and provision here on earth. When temptations would came, I would go to God's Word and say, "No, we have prayed the blood of Jesus over Jake. He is safe. God's Word is true."

I had several favorite verses, but I went often to Psalm 91. Jake wrote about one ambush they experienced when six men were shot by snipers. They were pinned down and had little cover. He said he had never been that frightened. He told us he prayed all night and read Psalm 91 over and over, putting in his name and the name of his company (see page 150 of this workbook). God was faithful. All of the men survived with no permanent wounds and all was well.

It was easier to pray for my son because I knew he also had faith and we were in agreement. If your son has a need and is not a believer, remember God loves an intercessor. Your prayers will be honored. Keep your loved one covered with prayer and know that God hears you. When we find ourselves in a difficulty, we must hold fast to God's Word and trust with all of our hearts...                    **[Psalm 91: God' Shield/ Military book, Testimony]**

### PRAYER from MARINE WIFE

My husband's unit was one of the first deployed into Iraq. One newscaster was following Jake's unit around everywhere they went and so much of the news was directly related to Jake and his fellow soldiers.
"I would have gone crazy watching the news every night worrying about Jake in those first few months of the constant reporting on the war in Iraq if that is all I had to rely on. Instead I had the promises of Psalm 91 to turn to!"                    **Jeanine Weise**

## PRAYER to STOP WILDFIRE

Last Thursday Taylor called me and said that he was at his ranch with his fire truck and that the wind was shifting 180 degrees and it was burning away from his house. I was very relieved until the next call about an hour later. He called his wife Kelly to tell her that the fire was a 50' tall wall of fire(4 miles long) and that he had done all he could but it was coming towards their home. He also said "It is just a house" and that they could replace it. Kelly relayed the message and I just got so frustrated. I tried to e-mail my Sunday school class to pray but the internet was down. Cathi said, "I started praying and opened my Bible to Psalms 91….all I had left was God. I started praying and reading His words of protection over us back to Him, reminding God of His promises. I saw on the television that the wind was 58mph so I just begged God – if you won't put out the fire could you just stop the wind and give Taylor a chance?" I was so worried about Taylor being between the house and the fire. I put up my Bible and cried, but, looked outside and within 5 minutes of my prayer, the wind stopped. It did not just slow down; it was **dead still.**

Taylor called in about an hour. The fire had burned **around** his house. I could not believe it! What a coincidence, the fire also burned around his shop and barn. The fire also burned around his hay bales. It also left two wheat fields that will be enough for his cattle to eat until the grass grows back. It did not hurt any of his cattle, horses or dogs. The fire also burned around his hunting cabin. Next to the cabin, it burned a dock all the way out in the water. I thought that was almost funny. And, by the way, Taylor took his truck about 2 miles down from the fire to save it. When he returned, the fire had burned over the top of his truck and not even hurt the plastic. His son's plastic slide in the backyard did not melt. Local fire departments were sent from many towns.

On the way to Ft. Worth I had listened to Robert Jeffress preach about Joseph. Robert said that God sometimes delivers us from adversity through the plea of others. I recently listened to Psalms 91 by Peggy Joyce Ruth from Brownwood as she explained all the protection God provides. If there was ever a day that I understood that God could protect us from anything it was that day. Just 19 days before the fire, Taylor had won the Texas Cattle Raisers award for Stewardship of his ranch. It was beautiful and the grass was tall. Taylor had created 22 water tanks, some of which were used by helicopters to refill their tanks and put out the fires. The fire burned several thousand acres and destroyed miles of fence. But it harmed nothing of Taylor's that was not replaceable. **In the few days since this dramatic fire I have asked myself – Did God answer my prayer?** *As for me and my house…*
*Testimony by Cathi Ball*

**On page 151 (his) and page 152 (her), it gives you the Psalm 91 scripture typed out to insert your name or your loved one in order to pray the covenant personally by name.**

# MOM and DAD'S PRAYER COVERING: PLANE CRASH

My son, Andrew, had recently returned from his second tour of duty in Afghanistan. This last one was one of those long 15 month tours with a year break in between. I spent many hours praying protection over him. Psalm 91 became particularly meaningful to me as I would pray this protection psalm over him on a daily basis. I would pray and thank God that "He would deliver him from the snare of the fowler," and that "He would give His angels charge over him to guard him in all his ways." It was such a relief this time when he returned because his active duty commitment to the Army was up and he was returning to civilian life.

As Andrew recalled the events of the day, he said he knew there was something wrong with the airplane when he heard a loud pop and then saw black smoke coming from the engine. As the plane banked to make a turn, Andrew reassured Stephanie, his fiancée, that it would be all right; they weren't far out from the airport and the plane was returning to land. As they looked out the window, Andrew realized there was a strange silence. Usually you can hear the hum of the engines, but he couldn't hear any engine at all so he realized they were only gliding. When they started losing altitude fast, he knew they were in trouble. At that moment the pilot came over the intercom and told them to brace for impact. Andrew knew they would be going down in the water, which somewhat relieved him that they would not be hitting land. He thought that might give them more of a chance for survival and that brought a spark of hope, mingled with fear. He was telling Stephanie that when they crashed, they would need to get off of the plane in a hurry. They kissed each other, said 'I love you', huddled close to one another and started praying together, as they braced for the impact.

Andrew said he had all kinds of scenarios running through his head in that one long minute they had before the impact. What if the plane tears apart and they get sucked down into the water. He knew he could possibly be frantically trying to find Stephanie. He also knew hypothermia could take over quickly and their lungs could freeze rapidly, along with their extremities. Andrew said he accepted that he was going to die and that he hoped to simply die upon impact rather than drown in freezing water. He told us that he also had the thought that he made it through two deployments to Afghanistan, and now it was going to end like this?

. We all praised God together and marveled at the miracle that had taken place. We rejoiced as Andrew witnessed how God was all over that flight…placing Chesley Sullenberger at the helm of the plane that day, the often busy Hudson waterway being clear of ferries, barges, and boats, keeping the plane in one piece and afloat while all 155 passengers were rescued, firmly planting their almost frozen feet on a slippery surface, in a swift current, and not allowing them to fall. Witnessing and experiencing this miracle first hand has certainly strengthened and affirmed Andrew's existing faith. Could it be that all those prayers, particularly the protection prayer of Psalm 91 prayed over Andrew

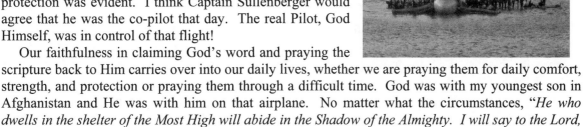

while deployed, continued to cover my son? Absolutely! He had survived two long tours of duty in Afghanistan and now upon his return, he is a survivor again. I believe the covering of mine and his Dad's prayers over our son helped carry him to safety that day. God's dramatic display of His protection was evident. I think Captain Sullenberger would agree that he was the co-pilot that day. The real Pilot, God Himself, was in control of that flight!

Our faithfulness in claiming God's word and praying the scripture back to Him carries over into our daily lives, whether we are praying them for daily comfort, strength, and protection or praying them through a difficult time. God was with my youngest son in Afghanistan and He was with him on that airplane. No matter what the circumstances, *He who dwells in the shelter of the Most High will abide in the Shadow of the Almighty. I will say to the Lord, "My refuge and my fortress, my God in whom I trust."* ------Mary Gray

# PERSONAL PRAYER: IMMINENT DANGER

Sgt. Tommy Brasington, Jr. from Toledo, MS,  decided to join the army after he worked with the families and survivors of the 9/11 tragedy. When he deployed to Iraq, several of his buddies had Psalm 91 written out on a bandana that they wore under their Army helmets to remind themselves and the devil that they were under the divine protection of God. Brasington said that when rocket propelled grenades begin slamming into your Humvee and roadside bombs are exploding all around, you need that continuous protection all over you. In this situation, it is not hard to obey the Biblical command to "pray without ceasing" when you know that apart from God's protection, your life could be over in a moment's time. Time after time he would be petrified with fear and then instinctively he would start praying Psalm 91 and strength and faith would immediately begin to rise in his heart.  There was no area where Brasington served, that the fighting was not extremely heavy:  in Abu Ghraib, in the rural area south of Baghdad and  in the middle of the city of Baghdad.

He knows that God has been His protection. In December his Humvee ran over a *roadside bomb* that sent the vehicle and its five occupants airborne.  It flew 300 yards, clearing a three-story building, and crashed down yards from the blast crater and continued to move (even though the tires were flat).  No one could believe that everyone in the Humvee was not killed instantly.  There was another brush with death when a six-year old Iraqi boy ran to warn them of a bomb.  They found that one, and four more, hidden behind the very gravel pile where Brasington and his buddies were hiding.  It was a well-planned ambush that should have taken all their lives, but God saved them.  They found out later that someone had pushed two detonator buttons to trigger the four bombs, but the detonator to one pair malfunctioned immediately and fuses leading to the other two bombs each stopped one inch short of the explosives. When the Army investigated, they said they could find no reason for the failures to detonate. What an awesome God we serve.

## JOURNAL IDEAS

1. A 50' tall wall of fire (4 miles long) coming straight toward Taylor's home (p. 84) ended with  the fire burning around his house, around his shop and barn, around his hay bales, around two wheat fields, around his cattle, horses and dogs, around his hunting cabin and over his pickup without harming it. Could Cathi praying Psalm 91 have had anything to do with something that supernatural?  This kind of praying has been referred to as praying "in proxy" for someone else?   There is an example of Jesus doing this in Matthew 8: 5-13.  *Have you ever prayed in proxy for someone?*

2.  In the plane crash (on page 85), Andrew's mother was praying protection over him daily. When the entire groups of passengers were saved, is this possibly the fulfillment of the scripture promise: *Your neighbor lives in the security of the believer? _____  (see related scriptures on page 92) . Have you ever been protected by someone else's prayer life or have your prayers covered someone else, as well?*

3. When Sgt. Tommy Brasington's Humvee ran over a *roadside bomb* that sent the vehicle and its five occupants airborne, flying 300 yards, clearing a three-story building, and crashing down yards from the blast crater, no one could believe that everyone in the Humvee was not killed instantly.  It was, however, no coincident that when Tommy deployed to Iraq, he and several of his buddies had Psalm 91 written out on a bandana that they wore under their Army helmets to remind themselves and the devil that they were under the divine protection of God. *How do you remind yourself daily of your Psalm 91 covenant?*

## CHAPTER TWELVE IN BOOK: ANGELIC PROTECTION

10. Write out Psalm 91:11-12 - _____
_____
_____
_____

11. What unique promise does God make in verses 11 and 12?

12. Who also used this promise and why?

13. When does the author think we will understand the magnitude of this promise?

14. What stories might we have read about this promise?

15. What does Hebrews 13:2 say?

16. How does the author explain verse 11?

17. If angels are taking charge of things, what does that mean?

18. If angels are taking _____ of the things that concern us, God has given the _____, not the _____, the authority to act on our _____.

19. What does Hebrews 1:14 say?

20. If we look to God as the Source of our protection and provision, what does it mean?

21. What else does verse 11 say?

22. What is the illustration the author used?

23. _____ is what releases this promise to work in our behalf.

24. Protection is not just an _____ in God's mind—He is _____ to it.

25. _____ protection is another one of the *unique* ways in which God has

_____ that _____.

## MAKE IT REAL: THE SPIRIT OF INFIRMITY AND FAMILY CURSES
Life Connection Parable

Patricia went to see her grandmother in the nursing home. As she listened to her grandmother catalogue all her aches and pains, illnesses and medications, Patricia felt a chill go up her spine. She had always been kidded about being a hypochondriac. And now she wondered if she really was, because with each description of a pain, Patricia had a sympathy symptom in the same place. Whenever she felt a pain, she would then worry that the illness would soon follow. It wasn't until a family reunion that weekend that Patricia began putting it all together. Her family had been plagued by illness. One of her siblings had died before she was born; fear of illness had swept through the family. The "other" children were heavily monitored for anything suspicious. Vacation plans were changed due to fear, sports were prohibited, the children were not allowed to play with other children who appeared to have illness, and the kids were taken to the doctor's office for the least little ailment. Patricia talked over family history with her relatives and the pattern was soon easy to detect. As the extended family began to list their medical histories, they realized they had experienced an abnormal amount of illness for any family: a child who was mentally impaired from a high fever, several cases of genetic birth defects, peculiar illnesses in every family member, accidents and regular visits to the ER clinic. Many of the family physicians would comment on the peculiar link that the family had to illness and harm, noting that it bordered on the bizarre. Patricia's husband, Ed, listened to his wife tell about her recent visit to the grandmother in the nursing home and the remark she wryly made, "I couldn't possibly have everything grandmother has, but I had a pain in the same area every time she talked about an illness!"

Ed thought about his own parents and brothers. When he grew up it was not random illnesses and accidents that plagued them like Patricia's family. It was a generational curse where the males had a tendency to die at a young age from heart trouble. Now that he thought about it, there was a clear pattern of the men dying before they had reached 60, many of them dying at the exact same age with each generation. After this enlightening discussion and Ed's own inner musings, no real conclusion had been reached, but it was obvious that collectively, the family had an abnormal disposition toward every imaginable sickness.

That night Ed decided to do something about it. He told Patricia about the early deaths he had observed in his own family. Combined with what he had heard of the constant illness in her family, he realized the kind of ramifications that could have on their growing brood. With their children, Ed and Patricia wrote out a covenant based on the Psalm 91 promise that no terror, no arrow, no pestilence, no destruction would come near their household. After they and the children read it together (some with a little help because of their age), they signed and dated it. Ed then prayed over each member of his family individually, blessing them with wholeness and rebuking fear and infirmity off his household. Then, in turn, Patricia and the children prayed over him that the male pattern of premature death would not come upon Ed or his children and that the Lord would satisfy him with a long life so he and his household could serve the Lord in their generation.

1. What patterns showed up in this family? Underline them in your workbook....

2. How did Ed properly handle the circumstances surrounding his family?

3. What would the outcome most assuredly have been if they had ignored the obvious?

 *Talk/Write about an experience where fear of illness attacked you. What did you do?*

The arrows below show a cycle of how the enemy gets his foot in the door and eventually brings John 10:10 into reality. Many times it starts with just a thought. Are you choosing to stop the enemy when you first recognize a negative thought or do you let that thought develop into something more? At which level are you putting a stop to his devices?

## Have you ever experienced this development?

**John 10: 10: THE THIEF COMES TO STEAL, KILL AND DESTROY,**
**BUT I HAVE COME FOR YOU TO HAVE LIFE, AND LIFE MORE ABUNDANTLY...**

**STARTS WITH A NEGATIVE THOUGHT**

**BEGIN TO FEEL SYMPTOMS**

**BLEAK SELF-DIAGNOSIS**

**FEAR OPENS THE DOOR**

**SICKNESS OR AN ACCIDENT OCCURS**

**RESULTS IN SOME SORT OF CHAOS**
**AT TIMES  LEADING TO DEATH OR DESTRUCTION**

## MAKE IT MINE: PATTERNS AND PRINCIPLES AND PRAYER
### Life Relevance Project

Talking Sticks add variety to group discussions. When a person holds the stick he has the floor. Also, it gives a tangible way to see that each person has a turn to speak. Use a talking stick/baton (or something that has special meaning or relevance to you) with your family or with the group to discuss patterns you have seen in your family of fatal diseases and accidents. Then talk about what Psalm 91 has to say about pestilence and accidents; and further discuss what can be done to put this part of the psalm into action. Give examples of times you have seen the power of God in action. This will give you an idea of the group's depth of understanding of the principles of protection. It will also introduce ways in which other people have found the psalm and promises relevant.

**SUGGESTIONS:** Start your child off early with his own copy of My Own Psalm 91 Book (for young children) or Psalm 91 for Youth. It is important to put this psalm in them at an early age and pray it over them from a preventative position.

**NOTE:** In the original Psalm 91 book, Peggy Joyce takes this concept about pestilence from the perspective of the Psalm 91 protection from illness and close brushes with life-threatening accidents. However, the Psalm 91 Military Edition is geared more toward accidents and acute danger.

# Us 4 & Let's Add Some More
To broaden your scope for more than just your immediate family—
here is another suggestion…

**Make a Prayer List** of family and friends over whom you can pray Psalm 91.

List times in the future when they might need Psalm 91 specifically, such as a vacation, plane trip, etc. When you have finished the list, make special prayer time to focus on Psalm 91 and pray it over those on your list. You can also fill out the Psalm 91 covenant in the back of this workbook with your friend's and families' names written right into the psalm.
Make a copy and mail it to each person on your list so they can be in agreement with the protection you are praying over them.

**Bible Interaction** (List other Scriptures that came to your mind which relate to this chapter) Joshua 24:15, Psalm 112:7, Matthew 4 :5-6, Hebrews 13:2, Hebrews 1:14, Joshua 2: 13, Matthew 13: 32, Psalm 103: 20

**Neighbors Live in the Security of a Believer: Luke 13:19; Acts 27:1-44; Genesis 14:1-16**

**Link to Last Week:** Thousands will be falling like flies all around me, but God warned me of this so that I would not be moved by it. (Adapted from Psalm 91: 7)

**Bait to Next Week:** I have been given authority over all the powers of the enemy. (Luke 10: 19)

## *Respond With Your Heart*

*How is household protection an advanced blessing from God?*

_____

_____

_____

*What area of household protection do I need to mature my faith in?*

_____

_____

_____

*How has my own faith developed as I believed for household protection?* _____

_____

_____

_____

*What part of my household do I need to give more control over to God?*

_____

_____

_____

# Journal

# LESSON ELEVEN: THE ENEMY IS UNDER MY FEET

### THEME: SCARY BEASTS REPRESENT THE FOUR TYPES OF ENEMY ATTACKS

## READ CHAPTER THIRTEEN

**Psalm 91:13:** "You will tread on the lion and cobra, the young lion and the serpent (dragon in the KJV) you will trample down."

### Points to Ponder

Read the analogy below or choose a volunteer to read the story aloud to the group. Answer the following questions.

## Interpreting Warning Signs

The cobra is the feared, deadly snake of a foreign land. It is known for its hypnotical swaying from side to side and its lethal venom.

However, in Texas, we have the rattlesnake. They are very proud of their presence and often announce their presence by a rattle of their tail. One night as we lay in our beds, we thought we'd left the lawn sprinklers on because of the racket outside. We found rattlesnakes lying on the cool tile of the porch rattling so loudly that we thought it was sprinklers going off in the night.

With certain types of problems there is a certain amount of warning first: lions roar, rattlesnakes rattle, and cobras flare their hoods. The most profound tool against these warnings is preventative prayer. Many people get a warning and just take it as a sign from heaven that something bad is going to happen and they simply let the calamity strike without any resistance.

My son-in-law recalls such an episode the night he was playing in a district game of high school football. Somewhere deep within himself, a voice said, "You are going to injure your knee tonight." Before the game was over, a clip occurred that damaged his knee so badly he had to have immediate surgery and was taken out of football altogether from his junior year on. He had to sit on the bench, inactive, as he watched his team go to state. This injury also kept him out of the marines when he tried to join a few years later. Now that he understands the power of preventative prayer against these subtle little warnings, he knows what to do.

While we were watching a family member's house burn, a neighbor came over and told my daughter, "I had a dream this house was going to burn!" Even at her young age, she rejected the notion that heaven had given the dream to the neighbor so he could brag that he had ESP; instead, she recognized it as a warning he could have handled in his prayer closet preventatively. People have different names for these warnings: *women's intuition, ESP, just a random instinct, a persistent thought,* etc. But, they are, in fact, warning flags in the spiritual realm. The devil likes to brag, criminals like to brag, rattlesnakes like to rattle before they strike and lions like to roar before they charge. Pay more attention to these subtle—and sometimes *not* so subtle—warnings and head off the attack with prayer.

1. Why is preventative prayer so effective?


2. Why is preventative prayer better than *after the fact* prayer?


3. What does preventative prayer do that no other type of prayer can?


# MAKE IT MEANINGFUL:
### Life Application Questions

1. Write out Psalm 91:13 - _____
_____
_____

2. Verse 13 goes from the subject of being protected to what new emphasis?


3. What New Testament scripture does the author refer to as corresponding?

4. We, as Christians, have been given _____ over the _____.

5. However, the authority over the enemy is not _____.

6. What does the author's husband say about the subject?


7. When we _____ the enemy-it is the time we need to _____ forth the _____ we have in the _____ of _____.

8. If we do not have that kind of courage, what should we do?


9. Most Christians, however, either do not _____ it or they fail to _____ it.

10. What are the Four Beasts of Psalm 91? _____, _____, _____, _____.

**4 TYPES OF DANGER**--You will TREAD on THEM (vs. 13)

These scary beasts—represent the 4 types of fears we face

        **Lion** {big bad, bold problems} Hits you in the face and blows your hair back.

                Defining moments are made when you defeat these problems…

      **Young Lion** {small bothersome irritating problems}

             Sent to harass you…the little foxes

      **Cobra** {sneaky and fatal} These sneak up on you and they are deadly

      **Dragon** {unfounded fears}

      No such thing…Have you ever had a fear that was totally ungrounded? _____

11. What are "lion" problems? List an example.

12. What are "young lion" problems? List an example.

13. What are "cobra" problems? List an example.

14. What are "dragon" problems? List an example.

15. What Old Testament verse does the author use to explain "dragon" problems?

16. What is the "Good News" regarding these problems?

17. God has given us His _____ of _____ and these problems now have to _____ to the _____ of His Name.

18. Why does the author like the word "tread"?

# THE FOUR TYPES of ATTACKS

**Draw or list the distinctions between the four types of problems represented by scary beasts. Name a related harassment in your life for each type of problem.**

| Lion<br>Bold problems | Young Lion<br>Harassment problems | Snake<br>Sneaky problems | Dragon<br>Fantasy problems |
|---|---|---|---|
|  |  |  |  |

**This is a very important section in this psalm about treading on lions, young lions, cobras and dragons. Until this point we were given promises. Now the Psalm shifts and it uses the words *"tread"* and *"trample"* to reflect authority. This portion tells you about the authority you have over your circumstances.**

**Name some times in the Bible where people used their authority?**

_____

_____

_____

_____

*Talk/Write about an experience where preventative prayer stopped an attack from the enemy in your life.*

# MAKE IT REAL:   ALL SIZES OF PROBLEMS...

Life Connection Parable

It was one of those days that just fell apart and unraveled at all the seams. Jeff woke up late after staying up into the wee hours of the night watching movies, grabbed a cup of coffee and rushed out the door, already fifteen minutes late for work. Since graduating, Jeff had not been able to quit living the college life at night and adjust to the early hours of adult responsibility by day. Prayer would have to wait. It was a day of that groggy feeling in the brain from too little sleep and too much rushing. Jeff worked for a church so they would excuse his tardiness.

Jeff had set up an appointment with a man who was living in the same region of South America where Jeff would be going on a summer mission trip. Just as he got to work late he remembered having made an appointment for an hour before work. But, at the moment, he couldn't remember who the appointment was with until he saw the note on his desk. Oh, just as well that he missed the appointment! There were a number of reasons why he should just give up on this trip anyway: his mom was afraid for Jeff to go overseas, even for two weeks; he had less than half of his money raised; he missed the last two fundraisers because of personal reasons; and he didn't like being away that long from Candace, the girl he was sure God had told him to marry.

Jeff snickered at the memo that no employee could use personal cell phones at work. *Was he the reason for the memo?* He would even agree that last week he had been on the cell phone too much—arguing with bill collectors, trying to straighten up a misunderstanding with Candace, and visiting with an old buddy who had come into town and was hoping to get a job at this same church with Jeff's recommendation. However, the cell phone wouldn't be a temptation this week since the cellular company had turned off his phone because of an enormous phone bill he had forgotten to pay. Life isn't fair, Jeff complained, because the biggest frustration of all wasn't his fault. Someone was running with his credit card and making charges at random gas stops and stores along the state lines. Having never had to deal with the confusion of bills, stolen identity and endless waits on hold with companies, he wished he were still a kid back at home. Well, maybe not! His sister had just been allowed to move into the house with her new boyfriend and the fighting was endless between his mom and step-dad.

Jeff was glad for his years at college, his degree and his new life. His roommate had shared Christ with him his freshman year and he'd made a 180 degree turn around. That roommate had been the accountability he had always needed, but college was over and each of them had gone different ways. Jeff realized that now was his time for growth, yet he was finding it hard to keep himself motivated. Never stopping to realize that his life had very little output, Jeff made a list of things to drop—the men's breakfast he had joined at church and the nursing home ministry he had started a few weeks before with a few volunteers he had recruited. This way he could put more time into Candace, who had just reminded him that he was late for their luncheon date.

Lunch was Jeff's one reprieve in this hectic day—his girlfriend was meeting him at their favorite spot and he could get everything straightened out between them. Then came the day's final blow! Jeff was not expecting Candace to be as nervous as she was, but suddenly, it made sense. Maybe he should have seen it coming. He realized now that she had arranged the lunch to break up in person.

Later when he saw the church secretary, she looked nervous too. Was Jeff just paranoid or did she look like she would rather be doing anything else? She dropped in on Jeff at the very end of the day to say that the pastor, who was also his boss, wanted to meet with him at 8:00 a.m. the next morning to discuss something important. Jeff wouldn't forget THIS early appointment. He comforted himself with the thought that maybe he was getting a raise.

1. Which of Jeff's problems were self-induced?


2. Which of the problems were legitimate which Jeff had no control over?


3. Jeff needs to conquer some bold problems, some daily problems, some sneaky problems and some fear problems: give an example of each from his life:


4. If he chooses not to take action, can you see his life becoming more hectic?


5. If Jeff doesn't preventatively pray against spiritual warfare, he could have a life blow that would knock him down in his walk with God, causing a terrible setback.
How could Jeff better handle the spiritual warfare on his life?


6. Do you think Jeff was getting a raise? _____ .

# MAKE IT MINE:  CONQUERED PROBLEMS
### Life Relevance Project


## Jesus Perez

   At sixteen I was wrestling with my religious beliefs.  My Jewish family had converted to Catholicism to avoid persecution…  I joined the army in 1998 and was sent to Korea.  I was still searching for my Jewish roots and it was there that I met some Korean Jews which was awesome.  While I was in Korea I was playing football.  I got tackled by two airmen and I fractured my back in three pieces.  I was taken to the emergency room and there I was told by the doctor, "Corporal Perez, I regret to inform you that you will never walk again."  That was devastating news for me because my dream had always been to be a chaplain since I was eight years old.  I stayed in the hospital, strapped in the bed, for about two to three weeks.  They were trying to decide what to do with me because I was no good to the army now.  They were going to send me home but I was needing some time to recuperate.  They did Xrays, MRIs and all kinds of medical procedures.  My L5 and S1 were completely shredded and I had no motion in my legs. It was just in pieces.  When the doctor told me that I was not going to walk again, I asked him, "Doctor, is this your professional opinion?"  He said, "Yes, it is."

So I said, "I have news for you. God has something else to say about this. I am trusting God to get me out of this bed because I want to be a chaplain and neither you , this fracture or anybody else is going to stop me." So that night was Sabbath and <u>I prayed, "If you are the powerful God of the Jews, and I am a Jew, I am asking that You perform in me the same miracles that you did for the people of the Bible."</u> I called the nurse and asked her to take the straps off of me and I asked her to take out the catheter. She said, "I will take if out, but don't do anything strange. I know you want to get out of this bed." She left and the man in the bed beside me was looking at me and he said, "What are you thinking?" I said, "I just want to go to the bathroom." So he said, "You can't leave the bed. You will fall." And I said, "No, I won't. I am going to go across the hall and go to the bathroom." So I got my legs off the side of the bed and I stood up and started walking down the hall." About that time he started hollering, "He's walking. Look at him. He's walking." The nurse came running and when she saw me walking, she said, "What are you doing?" They were all in an uproar. When I came out of the bathroom there was quite a commotion going on.

So they sent me to Japan to confirm that I did indeed have a fractured back. There was a nerve surgeon from the navy and when I gave him my X-rays and MRI he asked me, "Where is this soldier?" I said, "I'm right here, Sir" and he said, "No, don't play games with me because whoever these X-rays and MRIs belong to could not possibly walk."

1. Psalm 91 is one of the first glimpses of the authority of the believer in the Old Testament. This is a unique story of a Jewish army chaplain who claimed the miracles that God performed in the First Testament (as Jews refer to it) and received dramatic results from the hand of God. When there are New Testament Christians who do not know about their authority or Christians who have never one time used their authority over circumstances, this testimony shows clearly what they are missing out on. Look up Hebrews 8:6 and relate it to this story.

2. Jesus Perez faced a great crisis in his life that threatened to destroy his dreams. What did he dream of becoming?

3. Did Jesus Perez just accept the twist of fate that left him paralyzed as the working of God?

4. How did he use his authority?

5. How did he act on his faith once he prayed?

---

Have everyone in the group write a testimony of a time in his life when he faced a Lion (bold) problem, a Young Lion (gradual) problem, a Cobra (undercover) problem, or a Dragon (mirage) problem. Write how you turned to God in that situation and how God brought you out of that time of struggle. If you did not turn to God, write how you would handle things differently now. After each person has completed his testimony, staple them together to create a testimony booklet for the rest of the class to read. This would also make a good project to do as a family for a *family testimony book.*

# Bible Interaction

(Other Scriptures which relate to this chapter)
Luke 10:19, Song of Solomon 2: 15, Proverbs 28:1; 2 Corinthians 10: 4-5

**Link to Last Week:** I thank God that He made provision in my covenant for the safety of my family.

**Bait to Next Week:** God wants a personal relationship with me!

## *Respond With Your Heart*

*What is my first reaction when I encounter the enemy?* _____

_____

_____

_____

*Do I know when to take authority over the enemy as opposed to praying?*

_____

_____

_____

_____

*What area of my life do I need to walk in greater authority over the enemy?* _____

_____

_____

_____

_____

# LESSON TWELVE: BECAUSE I LOVE HIM
## READ CHAPTER FOURTEEN    THEME: RELATIONSHIP PROTECTION

Psalm 91:14a: "he has loved me, therefore I will…"

## Points to Ponder

**Read the analogy below or choose a volunteer to read the story aloud to the group. Answer the following questions.**

A young man in our college Bible study shared with me that he was feeling pressure from family and friends because of his zealous, passionate walk with the Lord. He was torn between the admonition of scripture to *honor your father and mother* and *he who loves his father and mother more than me is not worthy of me*! He wasn't the rebellious type, but struggled with a full time call on his life that he was ready to fulfill and he came to me to ask what he should do. I told him, "You are at a perplexing age—you are 19. You are on your own, but not quite. At 12, Jesus obeyed his parents. At 30, He followed God even when His mother didn't understand. You will have to decide for yourself. You are a man, but yet you are still to a certain extent under your parent's roof.  There is a cost to following."

 He said he needed a day to think about the cost.  Because I knew he was at the age to understand the pull of the female species, but perhaps not at the age to know whether he was ready to strike out on his own, I told him I had a story that I thought would help him understand the motive behind counting the cost.

> A young man at college took his girl out on a date. He had a good job and never minded spending money on himself, so he took her to the nicest steak restaurant in town. He was horrified when he purchased her a steak and she wasn't able to eat all of it.
>
> Afterward, they picked up his date's little sister who was visiting for the weekend, and they went to the ice-cream shop for a cone. He worried the whole time that her little sister would expect him to pay. But the sister paid for her own and offered to pay for her sister and his, as well.
>
> When he got home that night he hurried to let the girl out, because he had already spent too much time that Saturday night with her when he could have been studying. The whole week he had been agitated that she expected so much of his time. Without saying anything he had the impression that she wanted him to call her once a day, but he had other, more important things to do.

When I finished the story, I asked the young man, "Was this man in love with the girl?"  The young man replied a sharp, "No!"

Then I summed it up, "Yet the Bible gives us permission—no, actually *tells us*—to count the cost. But the truth is, when you are truly in love, the one you love means more to you than time or money!  If you always count what it costs you, you have never seen the value of what you are getting.  When love is there, the cost is inconsequential. That is the best way to know when you are ready to follow Him!"  Early that night he came back to my house and said, "I am a man and I am ready to follow!"

1. What things can hinder us from our walk with God without our even realizing it?


2. Which part of our lives is supposed to come first?


3. How can changing our priorities increase the intensity of our relationship with God?


## MAKE IT MEANINGFUL:
### Life Application Questions


1. Write out the first half of Psalm 91:14 - _____
_____

2. How does Psalm 91 change with verse 14?


3. What else is special about verses 14, 15 and 16?



4. Love is the _____ that binds man to God, and God will be _____ to His beloved. (Military)

5. True protection has everything to do with _____. (Military)

6. What does the author think should be asked of the reader?



7. Why is this important?

8. How does John 14:15 affect us as believers?

9. In these verses God makes seven promises. For whom are these promises reserved?

_____

_____

10. Our _____ is an extremely reliable *telltale* sign that shows us if we really love Him.

## HOW DO YOU TREAT SOMEONE THAT YOU LOVE? (Put a Y for yes and an N for no)

___be kind to them
___occasionally talk down to them
___want to spend lots of time with them
___treat them with respect
___tell others about how wonderful they are
___not think about their needs—after all they can believe God for what they need
___think of them often
___talk to them only once a week
___forgive them when they hurt you
___not know their likes and dislikes
___want to please them
___care about what is important to them
___listen to them
___talk to other people about the shortcomings you see in their life
___want to give them gifts
___being too preoccupied to listen carefully when they speak
___be happy when they are happy
___feel justified in keeping some things secret from them
___never lie to them
___share whatever you have with them

*Now, using a different color pen, on the same lines, write a "Y" if this is the way you respond to God and an "N" if it is <u>not</u> the way you treat God.*

Do your answers show that you treat God like someone you love? _____
Talk to God and tell him how you feel about Him.

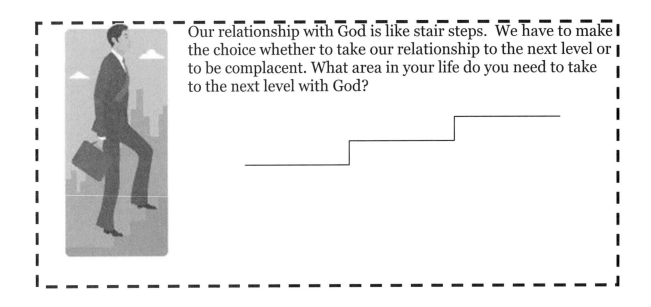

Our relationship with God is like stair steps. We have to make the choice whether to take our relationship to the next level or to be complacent. What area in your life do you need to take to the next level with God?

## MAKE IT REAL:    BY THE SKIN OF YOUR TEETH
Life Connection Parable

Brett decided he would put off having a relationship with the Lord. If he played his chances right, he could just slip in at the last minute like the thief on the cross. Something in Brett told him if he started serving the Lord, he would serve him fully and with his entire life. He just didn't know if he was ready to do that.

He had been thinking about this during a time when a couple of close friends passed away and he had a near miss himself. All of a sudden he realized how unpredictable life could be. Although he didn't realize it at the time, he was willing to give God his leftovers—the part of his life he had left when he was old and through living for himself. Yet these deaths left him feeling traumatized by life. When he passed a wreck on the drive home from work and saw the EMTs loading body bags, he winced inside.

However, something odd happened to Brett. It wasn't death that made him reconsider his plan. It was life. His dad called and asked him to go on a fishing trip in the Gulf of Mexico, all expenses paid. And his dad added, "Bring along Timmy, too." Brett had been careful to spend more time with his son, Timmy, than his dad had spent with him. Brett's dad was a traveling salesman during his younger years and had a lot more reasons to want to travel out of town than just the job alone. Brett had the feeling that it wasn't just earning a living for his family that drove his dad; it was a life where he could do as he pleased, sleep where he pleased and be whatever he pleased. His dad seemed to be full of regrets now—realizing a little late in life that what he missed out on was what really mattered and what would have really pleased him.

Brett agreed to the fishing trip and soon found himself immersed in hooks and bait and rolling waves. The three men challenged each other, making up their own tournament rules and lists of prizes. But at night, stories of childhood memories, family humor and future goals were talked over way into the night.

Strings of fish made the excursion a success, but there was another evaluation. Timmy summed up the trip so well: "Dad, the fun part was being with you."

That evening Brett got down on his knees and surrendered to God. It wasn't based on fear or the death of his friends, or calculating his chances of how close he could cut it, but it was based on how much time he would miss with his father… his heavenly Father. It was time that couldn't be made up.

Yes, he might avoid a lost eternity and a future in hell if later in his life he got it right with God. And, yes, time with his dad was precious at the end. But oh, the impact this fishing trip had made on him—causing him to recognize what he was losing now—the joy of living a full life in fellowship with God. Timmy made him realize what was already passing him by *NOW*! No more time to wait—it was time to get started!

1. What was Brett ultimately risking by putting off his relationship with the Lord?

2. How does Brett's relationship with his father and his son relate to his relationship with the Lord?

3. What finally made Brett realize what he was missing?

4. How could Brett remedy his situation?

# MAKE IT MINE: EVERY ONE DOES HIS PART
### Life Relevance Project

Psalm 91: 1-4: Our part: circle or highlight OUR PART in your study Bible:

( Say, ) ( Trust, ) ( May take refuge, ) ( Because he loves Me… )

Psalm 91: 5-16 God's part: underline GOD'S PART in your study Bible:
NOT ONE VERSE in this psalm says this HAPPENS for ALL CHRISTIANS!

# What are the Qualifications?

Fill in this chart with the corresponding verses from Psalm 91.
There are commandments (things we must do) with a promise attached to it. If a promise has a condition, we must be sure we are fulfilling the condition in order to receive the promise. The author notes that in verses fourteen through sixteen there are seven promises. Be sure and note that verses one through two give us clear commands with promises following. Verse fourteen makes a statement which describes our part before it states God's part.

| Commands, Principles, Truths | Promises Of God |
| --- | --- |
| | |

# Love Test

**Psalm 91: 14 Because he has loved Me, then I will....**

**Beside the excerpts and verses, write a number between one and ten—with #1 being "weak to non-existent" and then upward to #10 being "very heartily and fervently established".**

_____     Receiving His love gives us the capability to love Him back…

   (*see* I John 4: 19)

_____     If you love Me, you will obey me….
   (*see* Exodus 20: 6, Deuteronomy 5: 10, John 14: 15, John 14: 24, John 15: 10)

_____     Love Me with your heart   (*see* Matthew 22: 37)
_____     Love Me with your soul   (*see* Matthew 22: 37)
_____     Love Me with your mind   (*see* Mark 12: 30)
_____     Love Me with your strength   (*see* Luke 10: 27)

_____     If God were your Father, you would love Me [Jesus], for I came from God…
   (*see* John 8: 42)

_____     Who can say he loves God, but hates his brother…
   (*see* I John 4: 20)

_____     Do you love Me?  Then tend my lambs/sheep
   (*see* John 21: 15-17)

***Do we love God*** (according to how God describes *Love*)?

# Bible Interaction
(Other Scriptures which relate to this chapter)
John 21:15, John 14:15

**Link to Last Week:** I have authority over the works of the devil.

**Bait to Next Week:** Next time we will be looking at the benefits of our relationship with the Lord. When someone applies for a job, the person immediately likes to know the benefit package. Too many times we have tossed our manual aside and have never found out what God has already provided for us! Next week, we will discuss these benefits.

## *Respond With Your Heart*

*What am I doing to strengthen my relationship with God?* _____
_____
_____
_____
_____

*How has my relationship with God deepened as I turn to Him in times of need?* _____
_____
_____
_____

*Name some obvious and not so obvious ways in which God has provided for you.*
_____
_____
_____

# Journal

# LESSON THIRTEEN: God Delivers, Answers and Keeps Me
## READ CHAPTERS FIFTEEN THRU SEVENTEEN
### THEME: THE BENEFITS OF A RELATIONSHIP--HELP FROM ABOVE

Psalm 91:14b-15a: "...therefore I will deliver him; I will set him securely on high because He has known My name, He will call upon Me and I will answer him."

## Points to Ponder

**Read the analogy below or choose a volunteer to read the story aloud to the group. Answer the following questions.**

**ANGELIA'S STORY:** When my brother and I were fresh out of college we went on a family vacation. We stopped for the night at a large lake in Arkansas. Bill was feeling the strength of his youth and was very much in maximum physical shape when he challenged my husband to race him in a swim across the lake. Having 20/15 vision I could barely make out the bank on the other side of the lake and felt like Bill was misjudging the strength it would require to swim it on a whim. Being an adventurer myself I usually never let a challenge go unanswered, but I begged David not to do it, hoping that would hold Bill back.

Instead, Bill took off alone, despite my pleading. Stroke by stroke, we watched his steady arm motion carefully move him through the water, but halfway across, we realized he was in trouble. I was witnessing my brother drowning! Suddenly, something deep in me rose up as I determined not to be an only child. I prayed with all my strength. I did not want to cry out, because he was a little over halfway and I was afraid he would use all of his strength in an attempt to turn around if he heard me. David dove forward to swim after him, but I begged him to come back to take something that could float so they would not both drown together. I marked the spot and would not let my eyes deviate from where he went under so we could pull him up. He never came to the surface again where he went down in the middle of the lake. However, I set my faith; I would not lose my brother that day. And after what seemed too late, I saw his head re-appear out of the water closer to the bank on the other side about 40 to 50 feet from the opposite shore. A figure appeared on the other bank and threw something toward him, but missed him by a wide margin, and he went down again. This time when his head reappeared, he was in reach of the float.

By now the rest of the family had been alerted. We watched what appeared to be Bill lying on the bank. Sure enough, we drove around the lake to find Bill's body up on the shore of a grass-lined slope. The woman who threw the float told Bill she rarely went down to the water's edge as she had done this day. I ran over and asked Bill *HOW* he got to shore *under* the water. Bill said he felt all of his strength leave when he sank out in the middle and the sensation of drowning hurt as water filled his lungs. In the midst of his struggle, he said that he heard a voice ask him, "How much is your life worth?"

Bill, always the entrepreneur, answered with a monetary value--in the amount of a life insurance policy he had taken out on himself. Bill said that when he answered in a dollar amount, he forcefully went under the water again. The next time his head resurfaced he was nearer the bank and saw the lady as he was flailing in the water. She attempted to throw and widely missed. Once more, the voice asked him how much his life was worth, and again, Bill went under the water, but this time when his head emerged, he was in reach of the float. He has no explanation of how he went down in the middle of the lake and appeared near the shore. Each time Bill answered incorrectly with the same answer of his value in earthly terms, he would sink down under the water. Yet, he would miraculously resurface closer to the shore. When he emerged the third time, he relinquished, and seemingly gave the answer God was looking for. The lady verified that she missed him with her throw by a long shot. She could offer us no explanation of how he went under and then reappeared next to her float. Bill knew his life had been dealt with and spared, but it was a long time before he wanted near water again. I call this "the day I watched my brother drown" but God did a miracle before my eyes in that He didn't let it end that way. Psalm 91 promises are true, "therefore I will deliver him, I will set him securely on high, because he has known My name. He will call and I will answer him!"

#1 Have you ever been in a situation where only God could rescue you? Describe it!

#2 What was God apparently wanting from Bill?

#3 What kind of value would you answer to God that your life is worth?

 # MAKE IT MEANINGFUL:
### Life Application Questions

1. Write out the second half of Psalm 1:14:_____

_____

2. What is the first promise?

3. How does the author make it personal?

4. What are the two types of deliverance? (Military)

5. What question could we ask ourselves?

6. What is the answer?

7. In other words, God wants to deliver us from what?

8. Deliverance is all _____. It happens _____ (internal) and _____ (external); in fact, it _____ us. (Military)

9. What does Psalm 32:7 say?

## CHAPTER SIXTEEN

10. Write out all of Psalm 91:14: _____
_____
_____
_____

11. What is the second promise to those who love the Lord and know Him by name?

12. What other verses has the author found to support this promise?

13. What does the author tell us about the word "know" in the Old Testament?

14. How is the New Testament Greek different?

15. This promise of being seated securely on high is for the one who _____
    God _____.

16. What does verse 14 mean when it says "that we have known His name?"

17. What are some of the names and meanings?

18. Read Acts 4:12.

19. How is "saved" defined in Strong's Concordance? (Military)

## CHAPTER SEVENTEEN

20. Write out the first half of Psalm 91:15 - _____

_____ .

21. What is God's third promise?

22. Where is this promise repeated in the New Testament?

23. How does this promise affect the author?

24. What does Romans 10:11 say?

# Special Excerpt: GROUP PRAYER

As important as individual praying is, nothing seems to compare to leaders of a nation or a city or a group praying together in faith. When English soldiers were trapped at Dunkirk—with the German army behind them and the English Channel in front of them—the prime minister warned the nation that no more than twenty or thirty thousand of the two hundred thousand British soldiers could possibly be rescued from those exposed beaches. But no one could have estimated the power of a nation in prayer. The churches of England were filled; the king and queen knelt at Westminster Abby; the Archbishop of Canterbury, the Prime Minister, the Cabinet, and all of parliament were on their knees.

Four events happened in answer to prayer: First, one of the Nazi generals decided to regroup and ordered a halt of the German troops when they were only twelve miles away from Dunkirk. Second, Hitler made a rash decision to hold them there indefinitely. Third, the weather suddenly proved to be a great hindrance to the enemy planes firing on the English who appeared to be trapped like mice on that French coast. Finally, every imaginable vessel that would float–everything from private boats piloted by bank clerks, fishermen, Boy Scouts, yachtsmen, barge operators, college professors, and tug boat captains—started their daring rescue missions of the men trapped on the shore. Even London fire brigade boats got in on the action. Ship yards were quickly set up to repair the damaged vessels so they could return for another load. Anyone would have said the undertaking was absurd, but the **prayers of a nation** prevailed in one of the most dangerous and seemingly impossible endeavors in history.

On the boats taking them to safety, the men began to pray—many of whom had never prayed before. At the military camps in England the men requested permission to pray. It became apparent to all of Britain that their prayers were being heard. More than 7000 troops were evacuated the first day; 47,310 the second day; then, 53,823, next 68,014, and finally 64,429 in the next three days, respectively. In total, there were 338,000 British, Belgian and French troops brought to safety.

Collective prayers were being called for on both sides of the ocean at strategic turning points of the war. President Franklin Roosevelt issued a proclamation for prayer; and a nation responded.

When we think of the power of individual prayer, let's not forget history's record of what happens through corporate prayer. When a nation prays, when a city prays, or when leaders pray—it strengthens the individual's prayer. When people call upon God—He answers. When nations call upon God— history records the results.

How could you be *a part of* or *help initiate* a unified appeal to God for His help?_____

_____

Do you have any special reflections on this excerpt on *Collective* praying: _____

_____

_____

_____

Write out a time when you were involved in group prayer:_____

_____

# MAKE IT REAL: WHEN YOU MAKE A PROMISE

### Life Connection Parable

Grandpa Morton was of the old school of thought. A man was only a man inasmuch as he kept his word. He drilled this into his grandchildren. After the heat of the midday settled down to a mere meltdown and the locusts were running their chainsaw-like cries—logging in their own personal complaints about the temperature, you could find Grandpa sitting on the front porch spitting sunflower seeds or eating ice cream with a fork out of his tin coffee cup. Grandfather worked hard all of his life and was known for the help he gave to his neighbors. He was generous with his time and his money and had a infectious laugh. People wanted to be around him, but when he wasn't around, people talked about him: how he slipped them some money when they had a hardship in the family, how he tended to their farms when someone was down in their back, how he painted the widow's home, and how he relentlessly picked up the town drunk each Sunday to take him to church.

One day when I came running up to the house, Grandpa Morton was lying on the ground clutching his heart. It looked like he was gone. I can't remember what happened next in the pandemonium that followed, but with the aid of others, we got him to the hospital. I couldn't stand to see him in that kind of pain. Soon, the doctor who was on duty called us in for our last goodbyes. I wasn't ready to let him go and told him so. My tears dried up when he told me to voice a prayer to heaven. I made God a promise, right then and there; if He would let Grandpa Morton live until I married and he could see my children, I would commit my life to Him. Various pictures of service swept over my mind—everything from preaching in the county jail every Friday night to missionary work in huts in some remote part of Africa. I don't know if what I did would fit right in a theology book on *Bargaining with God*, but it was all I could think of at the moment. And Grandpa miraculously lived. I have pictures of him holding my first son and the daughter who followed two years later —as he sat on the porch, spitting out sunflower shells.

Perhaps, that's why I chose to be a chaplain when I went into the military—so I could share my faith with men who never had a Grandfather Morton. And yes, I've been to those places with huts and natives, I've parachuted with the men I serve on dangerous missions and I've told them that a real man is a man who keeps his word…because we serve a God who keeps His!

1. Why is it important for us to trust God in difficult situations such as this one?


2. Did the man live up to his end of the bargain?


3. Have you ever made a bargain with God?


4. Did you keep your end of the promise?


*Talk/Write about an experience where you made God a promise.*

## MAKE IT MINE: ARE YOU A MAN OF YOUR WORD?
### Life Relevance Project

God so faithfully keeps His promises, but have we kept ours? A number of Iowa's 113th Cavalry—an outfit that fought superbly in the European war—received Easter cards that opened their eyes. The front of the card included a sketch of a German battle field labeled *Easter, 1945.* On top in large letters was the question "*Remember?*" On the inside of the card was a family fireside sketch and the following: "*Well, God DID what you asked! He delivered you safely home and set you back on high. Now, have you done what you promised? How about Easter, 1950?*" The card was signed by the Reverend Ben L. Rose, pastor of the Central Presbyterian Church, Bristol, VA. This pastor should know their promises—**he was the chaplain** of the 113th Cavalry.

Many times in dangerous situations we make God promises—foxhole commitments! What a reminder! Do I sincerely love Him? This chaplain wanted to make sure his men remembered their vows. Do I really know Him by name and trust in His promises? *Have I been faithful to keep the promises I've made to Him?*

*If this story triggers a memory of something you vowed to God, do the following:*

---

**1ST SUGGESTION:** Design a card like Chaplain Ben Rose sent to his men, but make it to Yourself to help remind you of promises you made to God when you were in trouble and called out to him:

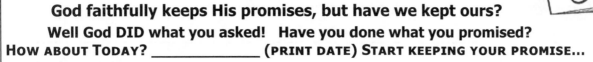

## God faithfully keeps His promises, but have we kept ours?
### Well God DID what you asked! Have you done what you promised?
**HOW ABOUT TODAY?** _____ (PRINT DATE) START KEEPING YOUR PROMISE...

**Author's example:** Ron Lantz, the truck driver who nabbed the snipers (page 69) had promised his dying son that he would commit his life to serving God and had been very faithful to that promise. He had been delivering food in the snow, distributing clothing and school supplies to needy families, leading the men's ministry and teaching Bible classes. Then God used Ron to stop two madmen.

**Another example:** Art Clifton almost died on the operating table. In that brief second while he hung between death and life, he made God a promise: "I'll serve you faithfully if you will let me live!" Art kept that promise. He and his wife drove hours to be a member of our TYC prison Bible study team. When they moved 3 years later, they found the local prison in their area and continued the promise. We would often joke with Art—he started volunteering in the prison ministry *so soon* after his operation—his stitches were still wet!

---

**2ND SUGGESTION:** Plan a Walking Talk:

Team up with a family member or close friend. If you need to get some things right with the Lord, set aside an hour to go walking with this close friend and talk about it. Maybe there are some promises you have made or some promises you need to make. (Some might need to talk with God alone and use their special prayer walk to work out specific issues that are on their hearts.) Then ask the Lord how to get started and make that first phone call.

**Bible Interaction**
(Other Scriptures which relate to this chapter) Joel 2:32, Psalm 32: 7,
Luke 1:37, Ephesians 1: 20-21; 2:6, Hebrews 8:11, Genesis 22:14, Acts 4:12,
1 John 5:14-15, Romans 10: 11

**Link to Last Week:** The seven bonus promises at the end of Psalm 91 are made to those who genuinely love the Lord.

**Bait to Next Week:** Next week we will take a look at the next set of promises that God makes to those who love Him. Included is a special section on the seduction of the spirit of death. When we talk about the promise of long life it is important to know that death comes to try to steal this promise, and the manner in which death does this is not the way we would expect it to come.

## *Respond With Your Heart*

*What specific provisions has God promised me?* _____
_____
_____
_____
_____

*How do I show my appreciation to God's provision?* _____
_____
_____
_____
_____

*Name a time in my life when God specifically kept me safe.*
_____
_____
_____

# Journal

# LESSON FOURTEEN:
## GOD RESCUES US FROM TROUBLE AND HONORS US
# READ CHAPTERS EIGHTEEN-NINETEEN
**Theme: Benefits of Relationship: Help for earth**

Psalm 91:15b -16a: "I will be with him in trouble; I will rescue him, and honor him…"

### Points to Ponder

*As Paul Harvey would say, "Now for the rest of the story…"*

I would like to share this story of the tornado—relating it from our perspective as teens who grew up in a home where we were taught Psalm 91 from a young age.

When my parents had me go outside and speak to a tornado, I realized I didn't have normal parents. It dawned on me when parents would put their children outside quoting God's word in the face of a storm, they must really believe the stories in the Bible. The radio warned us that the tornado was headed straight for our house. I could feel faith rising in my heart as my parents put us in a position to put our faith in action. I know this seems strange, but it actually made my faith go to a higher dimension when my parents involved Bill and me in this bold action of speaking to the storm. I *knew* they loved me, I *knew* they wanted us to be protected, I *knew* they believed what the Scripture said (even more than what fear was saying) and I *knew* they had set the course of action for the family that night to bring about protection.

We were in our pajamas with some friends who were spending the night as Mom and Dad led the family in our stand on the scripture. Just as Jesus spoke to the storm, "Peace be still!" we were going to speak to one ourselves. I realized this was actually a test of how much of the Word of God we had hidden in our hearts. For the first time, I realized that I didn't have Psalm 91 memorized and being in the middle of the ominous scene didn't make it any easier. I had to repeat the words after my parents. What a faith builder it was for us when that tornado lifted back into the sky and disappeared.

This story has always fascinated people—my professor at school the next day, people who hear the story on Mom's radio program and even people who read it in the book still ask me questions about that night. While others hid in bathtubs with mattresses piled on top of them or locked themselves in closets for hours, Mom and Dad took us to the only thing which was undeniably secure—God's Word!

As told by Angelia Ruth Schum

1. Why was it important for Angelia to be standing on her own faith?

2. Would you agree that memorizing Psalm 91 might come in handy?

## MAKE IT MEANINGFUL:
### Life Application Questions

1. Write out Psalm 91:15 - _____

_____

2. What is God's fourth promise?

3. Human nature cries out to God when _____ with _____. (Military)

4. If a person never felt danger, he never thinks about what? (Military)

5. We have to _____ in _____ and not confine Him to our _____ _____.

6. What does Isaiah 43:2 say?

7. The world calls happenings like these a coincidence – what does the author call them?

# How Often Do We Seek God?

| TIMES WE SEEK GOD: | LIST AN EXAMPLE FROM YOUR LIFE: |
|---|---|
| When we are happy | |
| Thanking God for an answered prayer | |
| Appreciation for something special from God | |
| Acknowledging God in everyday life | |
| Stagnant times in life | |
| Seeking God in times of need | |
| Depending on God during hard times | |
| Turning to God in times of trouble | |
| Other: | |

8. Man turns to God in both good and bad times. Think of times in your life when you turned to God during difficult experiences and during triumph.

9. Since this Psalm covers scriptures for both extremes do you tend to turn towards God in happy times or in difficult times?

## CHAPTER NINETEEN

10. Write out Psalm 91:15-_____

_____

11. What is the fifth promise to those who love the Lord and know Him by name?

12. What were some examples highlighted by the author of being honored?

13. How do we enable God to honor us?

14. How does God honor us?

# MAKE IT REAL: LETTING GO AND RELEASING FAITH
Life Connection Parable

The door slammed as my son, John, left the house. Immediately, I felt that familiar pain in the pit of my stomach as the car backed out of the driveway. He was leaving again. It seems that life is a series of steps of different degrees of "letting go".

It began when my spouse had left the family with no warning before John began school. I think the reality of divorce intensified the feelings of being left alone. The first time John had left for the summer to work for his uncle to earn some extra money, I began to dread the day John would leave for good. It seemed like I was fighting for my life—proud that John was a good kid and that he wasn't afraid of work, but heartsick at the thought of what life would be like without him around.

It was in the daily devotional on my computer that morning that I read Genesis 22 where it says Abraham took his son—the thing that meant the most to him—to the altar. I could identify with what Abraham felt, knowing that his son was a gift from God, but yet having to release him. It was then that God graciously gave Isaac back to his father. Abraham probably never struggled with releasing Isaac again since he had passed the hardest test of all on that mountaintop. In many ways that story reflected my own journey. Summer jobs took John away, but so did college. Then, again, John quite unexpectedly left our "family" summer plans, the time he went on a mission trip for the summer in a place most would consider a very dangerous area. With other parents refusing to let their children go, I let my only son go, and with my blessing.

But today was different. He wasn't leaving for a short-term summer mission trip; John had said goodbye as he left for his deployment. He was a chaplain and he was ready to go where few others would even dare to go. He had sought out what he thought was the toughest branch of the military and had joined a handpicked group of men who had one of the most dangerous assignments the military hands out. John had told me in high school he wanted the discipline that the military offered, but he also wanted to influence soldiers who were facing the most challenging moments of their lives. Until John had children of his own, he would probably never know what that does to those back home who love him. It is our toughest challenge.

So what did I do? I did what I have always done. When I heard that friendly goodbye and the door slam, it was not time for me to fall apart. I walked over to my Bible, picked it up off the arm chair and read out loud that well-worn page of Psalm 91. John's grandfather had shared with him that he had fought through an entire war carrying that psalm. In fact, I'd already penned John's name in the margins of my Bible. "John dwells in the shelter of the Most High and He abides under the shadow of the Almighty…" My voice had begun to pick up confidence as I read those verses. Thoughts of tormenting fear were replaced with Biblical images of shields and fortresses, wings and angels. "With a long life I will satisfy John, and let him behold my salvation."

I found John's newly-purchased deodorant where he left it on the back of the sink, and I laughed to myself. John may not smell so good, but he had remembered what was most important—he had his shield. As we had said our earlier goodbyes, John proudly showed me he had not forgotten his own personal copy of Psalm 91—the one his grandfather had given him.

1. How was John's mother able to let her son go with comfort?

2. How does the story of Abraham and Isaac relate to this mother and son?

3. How did this mother make the covenant of Psalm 91 personal for her son and his situation?

 *Talk/Write about an experience where you felt protected from danger.*

## MAKE IT MINE:   HELP ON EARTH—PASS IT ON!
### Life Relevance Project

**Think of someone who is going through a struggle right now in his or her life.  Then think of some way you can help or encourage that person this week. List your ideas below and then follow through with one or more ways so you can be an encouragement and a blessing to someone in need!**

- ☐ Write an encouraging note
- ☐ Volunteer to be a set of ears they can talk to
- ☐ Make a list of Bible verses to help their situation
- ☐ Pray with them about their problem
- ☐ Sponsor a child by giving up cold drink/snack money/loose change
- ☐ Mentor a child who has lost a parent
- ☐ Ask your spouse for something special you can do for him or her
- ☐ Write a letter to a soldier—especially on holidays

**Pray that God will turn around that person's situation and that He will use you to be an encouragement and inspiration to others in need.**

# Bible Interaction
(Other Scriptures which relate to this chapter)
Isaiah 43:2, Ecclesiastes 11:9, 20

**Link to Last Week**: I am seated on high with Christ. Satan is under my feet.

**Bait to Next Week**: Is just having a lot a birthdays a good thing, or does God make us an extra promise about our life in Psalm 91?

## Respond With Your Heart

*Do I seek God in both good and bad times?* _____

_____

_____

_____

_____

*How can I be more appreciative of the goodness of God?*_____

_____

_____

_____

*In what ways can I let my life be an example of Jesus to others?*

_____

_____

_____

_____

_____

*How can I benefit from memorizing God's promises?*

_____

_____

_____

_____

# Journal

# LESSON FIFTEEN: SATISFIED WITH LIFE!
## READ CHAPTER TWENTY

Psalm 91:16b: "With a long life I will satisfy him…"

**Points to Ponder**

When the people hear you say that you are going to live a long life, do they inadvertently groan? Or, do they immediately get happy because of the difference your life makes to everyone around?

Recently, I heard a true story about a grandfather who, upon his deathbed, spent an hour talking with his granddaughter. A certain mischievousness united the two. However, when she didn't think she could bear his departure, even at such a ripe old age, he sang her a song that went something like this: "I've never been so homesick in my life. I'll see you on the other side of the Jordan." She cried as he sang her the soulful gut-wrenching words of departure. And with that song sung to her, he died.

It is worth noting not only how a person dies, but also how he lives his life. One older gentleman admitted that he wanted lots of tears around the casket, but he had saved and saved to make sure that each family member's tears would soon turn to joy at the reading of the will. He said he would make sure that the proverb came true in his family, "A good man leaves an inheritance for his children's children."

Another lady, who was approaching golden years herself, told about her grandmother's lasting effect on the family. The grandmother through the years constantly slipped her money and would tell her, "You are my favorite! Now, don't you tell any of the others, you hear?" At the graveside, each of the seven grandchildren cried his heart out. It wasn't the sorrow of bitterness, but sorrow that comes with deep passion. One family member said, "I can't quit crying, I was the favorite, you know." The ones standing near stopped their weeping, to argue, "No, I was the favorite, she told me so!" Gradually they put it all together. As each told fond memories, it was clear grandmother had been for years telling each one of them that he or she was the favorite. Everyone was surprised that grandmother had gotten by with this for all those years, with so many grandchildren, but each of them had a good laugh at the end. For each had had value placed on his life from the love of this good woman.

I can't stop without adding a memory of my maternal grandfather who left me a good spiritual inheritance. He was a good Baptist man who loved the Lord. Often he would get up and turn on gospel music early in the morning and "shimmy," as he called it, to the Lord's music. It was his own version of King David dancing before the Lord. Not too many years after he died, I was pulled aside by a deacon in his little country church who said, "Your Grandfather, Ruby Smith, was known as the last man who shouted in the church!" Perhaps he shouted when he sang, or maybe when he *amen'd* the preacher. But I do know one time that he really shouted. Granddad had been trying his best to get the town drunk saved. Finally, he offered him a night of coon hunting with his hounds if he would attend church the next morning. That next day, the town drunk made his way to the altar and gave his heart to the Lord. They said Grandpa started shouting at the back of the church and all the way to the front. He also didn't bother to use the aisle in that rural church—he came right over those pews, clear to the front. Maybe that was the day he got the reputation of being the last man to shout in church! That story was a better heritage than a large perishable inheritance.

#1. Will the preacher have to lie about how you lived your life in order to give you a decent burial?

#2. What are some fond memories that your family has of you?

#3. It is not too late to start making memories. What could you do to strengthen your relationships with your loved ones?

The concluding promise of this magnificent psalm of protection ends with one regarding length of life, however, this isn't the total story. The psalm has painted a picture of a life well-lived—a life of one who has loved God, and a life that has found satisfaction. A preacher once said: "The Best Testimony to Jesus Christ is a Satisfied Customer!"

1. What kind of stories will your grandchildren know you by?

2. Write a short mock obituary of the life you want to achieve.

## GUIDELINES FOR WRITING A CHRISTIAN OBITUARY ABOUT A LIFE WELL LIVED:

- WRITE A SUMMARY OF THE ESSENCE OF THE PERSON
- DESCRIBE EARLY CHILDHOOD MEMORIES
- TELL ALL VITAL INFORMATION OF THE PERSON'S FULL NAME, OCCUPATION, HOBBIES, HOME CHURCH, SURVIVING AND DECEASED RELATIVES, AND HOBBIES.
- WRITE A PRAYER OR SCRIPTURE VERSE
- DESCRIBE THE PERSON'S CONVERSION AND IMPORTANT HIGHLIGHTS OF THEIR FAITH
- TELL FOND MEMORIES
- SHARE FAVORITE QUOTES
- WHAT WOULD THE PERSON MOST LIKE TO BE REMEMBERED FOR?

## MAKE IT MEANINGFUL:
### Life Application Questions

15. Write out the first part of Psalm 91:16 - _____
_____

16. What is the sixth promise?

17. Some people may say having a great many birthdays is not necessarily a blessing. How does this promise differ?

18. There is a *God shaped* _____ on the inside of each one of us.

19. Man has tried to fill that vacuum with many different things, but nothing will satisfy the emptiness until it is filled with _____.

20. What is the offer God is making?

## CLAIM THE PROMISE OF: SATISFACTION and LONG LIFE?

| CATEGORIES TO GAUGE SATISFACTION : | LIST AN EXAMPLE FROM YOUR LIFE: |
|---|---|
| A satisfying relationship with the Lord | |
| Provision for your daily needs | |
| Appreciation for Special Prayer Answers | |
| Acknowledging God in everyday Aspects of Life | |
| Fulfillment in Purpose and Ministry | |
| Satisfying Relationships | |
| Special Moments in Life | |
| Your Contribution to Others | |
| Good Surprises & Happy Occasions | |
| Other: | |

# Special Excerpt: Death Comes With a Pretty Face!

God promises us long life, but we have to receive it. We can't flow with what feels good and win this battle of life over death because the enemy will make the wrong path extremely easy to take.

Ed Rickenbacker, a famous flier in both World Wars, said, *"I felt the presence of death, and I knew that I was going. You may have heard that dying is unpleasant, but don't you believe it. Dying is the sweetest, tenderest, most sensuous sensation I have ever experienced. Death comes disguised as a sympathetic friend. All was serene; all was calm. How wonderful it would be simply to float out of this world. It is easy to die. You have to fight to live. And that is what I did. I recognized that wonderful, mellow sensation for what it was—death—and I fought it. I literally fought death in my mind, pushing away the sweet blandishments and welcoming back the pain. The next ten days were a continuous fight with the old Grim Reaper, and again and again, I would feel myself start to slip away. Each time I rallied and fought back, until I had turned the corner toward recovery."*

Captain Rickenbacker should know! Death certainly came toward him many times as a soldier in both World Wars, a survivor of two plane crashes, lost for 24 days on the Pacific…

It is these inner dynamics at work when a person is wounded, facing a serious illness, wracked by pain from an injury or sensing impending doom. Sometimes the spirit of death actually makes a bid for one's very life. It is easy to give in to it. We think of the ugly side of destruction, but the danger is when it comes with a pretty face. It is a fight to break free from the enticing call of death and push through to victory and life.

*How did Captain Rickenbacker describe death—as pleasant or unpleasant?*_____
*This is very important to know so that we resist death when it comes like an angel of light. ( 2Corinthians 11:14)*

*Death is crafty. Name some of the words he used to describe death:*

*Have you ever had a similar experience or known someone who has?*

*How did Captain Rickenbacker fight back? (see complete story in chapter 15 and chapter 20 in Military book)*

*SIDENOTE: Did you know that the mayor of New York asked the entire city to pray for Captain Rickenbacker's safe return? [Military book, Chapter 17]*

# Resisting Death

Commander John Quarrie, a WW2 submarine commander, voiced a similar commentary about the appeal of death: Quarrie was deep under the surface of the water after his ship went down, and a great temptation came over him to just let go. His whole body was full of pain, for he had wrenched his back badly, and he felt he could not swim. He wanted only to drift and sleep. But he tried to prod himself, realizing, he said, that this was only "an argument inviting and consenting to death, when the world needs men who are alive and can fight."

The battle then, he told his biographer, was terrific. It was a double fight, with the water, of course, and also within his own mind which seemed so numbed that he wanted only to stop thinking and give up. But he kept rousing his mind, as best he could, and trying to make his mind rouse his body so it would swim.

*How did Commander Quarrie describe the sensation of death?*

*His mind wanted to sleep, but he made his mind rouse his body. Have you had this sensation before?*

# "I Wish I Had Found Out About Psalm 91 Years Ago!"

**Fill in your personal story:**

**What I would like to say to people who have had a horrible tragedy**: God loves you. He never intended for you to come into that kind of hurt. His word is true and He is offering you these miraculous promises so you can crawl up into His Hiding Place. I would never attempt to offer any kind of explanation of what went wrong (I don't think any human could). One may possibly never know, for sure, what happened in the past that opened a door or if unexpected things just slipped in but I believe that we can start today and appropriate the promises to prevent future tragedies. When there are things we don't understand, we can concentrate on the things that we do understand: the compassion of God and the fact that He is for us and not against us.

First, I always approach the study of Psalm 91 as full of promise for **present and future**. Scripture is never meant to bring condemnation and I would steer a group study into a look at Psalm 91 as a *preventative* scripture for the future rather than a look of *regret* at the past. As far as the context of Psalm 91 goes, this passage doesn't address what to do in the case of something that has already gone wrong. To stay in the context of this passage, I did a verse by verse in depth look at what you can enjoy from this day forward.

ASSURANCE OF PROMISES: "Victories I've had in the past give me faith for the problems I face today!" One of the most reassuring foundations a person can have is past testimonies where they can look back and see the faithfulness of the Lord. However, many people may be starting on their faith walk brand new to all the promises. This is exciting as they see the promises work in their lives and acquire past victories to help them have faith for the future.

**THE PAST:** "I really regret that I have never before seen all these promises. I wish I had known about Psalm 91 earlier in life."

**THE PRESENT:** "I want a fresh start with Psalm 91 promises today!"

**THE FUTURE:** "I don't want to let what has happened in the past stand in the way of the future."

# When Tragedy Has Already Happened!

Peggy Joyce tells this story in her own words:

*"My father died young. He had just been saved and was on fire--witnessing up a storm when a young kid who had emotional problems came into my parent's home and set their garage on fire, burned up their truck and most of their home. When my dad saw the damage, he just gave up and wanted to go home. Most people never knew that was his attitude because he started working on the house and kept busy, but within six months he went home at age fifty-seven. It devastated our family because we were just coming into understanding the promises and knowing that healing was available. What is odd, during the 8 years while I was in depression, I feared my dad's death. [see* **Tormented: 8 Years and Back** *for Peggy Joyce's testimony of deliverance from torment.] But after it happened, God led me to make a quality decision that I would not let his death keep me from trusting the promises. Now, I look back and see what I would have missed out on if I had walked away from believing that the promises are for now."*

*#1   Death can come in as an offer of escape or as an outlet for hurt or pain. When should you resist death?*

*#2   Sometimes even those closest to a person don't know whether the person is honestly resisting it. Others are obviously crying out for help, looking for avenues of escape, fighting depression and openly expressing dark thoughts. Have you ever sensed this on someone?*

*#3   What choice does a decision for an early death leave for those left behind?*

**As far as terrible tragedies which have happened in the past, it is good to remind ourselves of these truths:**

## #1 God never desires the death of anyone (Ezekiel 18: 32). God never desires the death of the wicked (Ezekiel 33: 11). Therefore, knowing for sure that if He doesn't even will the death of someone like Hitler, He certainly does not will the death of our loved ones, innocent children or Christians in general.   The Bible never calls death a friend, but an enemy, and a <u>final</u> enemy in I Corinthians 15:26.

## #2 Death Stings.   God is full of compassion. And the best we could possibly know about how He feels is to see how Jesus handled death. You see Jesus weeping with us in John 11: 35. We see the compassion Jesus demonstrated in Luke 7:11-17 when He stopped a funeral because He saw that the dead boy was *the only son of a widow*…in other words, he saw the agony of the mother. He responds to us. If God had caused or willed the death, Jesus would not have been resurrecting dead people. Every incident from Jesus demonstrates the very heart and compassion of our Father.

## #3 We are in intense Spiritual Warfare and there is no real or lasting protection **outside the promises.**   In Daniel 10: 12-13, 21-23, it lets us know that behind our prayers there is much warfare that goes on.  And we know that over time, it has even intensified like birth pains. Revelation 12:12  tells us that in the last days the devil's wrath is even greater because he knows his time is short. This is not a fictitious warfare, but a real danger we can't see with our physical eyes.

## #4   Death as a Sacrifice [Read *We are so Grateful to you, Our Military*, Military Book]
Hebrews 11 refers to the faith of all these people who have had great protection and rescues but then the author mentions a special class of people who are martyrs. There is no contradiction between the martyr verses and the protection verses.  The writer of Hebrews 11 could not have said it any better when he tagged them as those—for whom the world is not worthy….!!  The Bible that we enjoy came at a great cost and many chose a martyr's death rather than deny the truth.  Yet, we see scriptures concerning  martyrs and the recognition of the sacrifices they have made and we often don't stop to realize that this is different than being randomly murdered, or killed by an accident or having a wasted life because of squandering our time or having our life cut short by a tragedy. There is a difference between being murdered and being martyred. Revelation 12: 11 *"and they overcame him by the blood of the lamb, the word of their testimony and they loved not their life even unto death"*—lets us know that there are some things more important than even life.

**#5 Persecution and Suffering** is greater in some areas of the world than in others and the protection promises of Psalm 91 work for them, as well, if they know to use them. There is a strong difference between random acts of violence which catch us off guard and have no redemptive purpose, and in the call of evangelizing or taking the gospel into dark places where people have sometimes laid down their lives as an act of love. This type of death has a purpose, a signing of our testimony in blood. According to Matthew 26:53 we see how Jesus knew He had protection (a great deal of it) but chose not to use it because He purposed to lay down his life. Yet before the time of the death on the cross when "He chose to lay His life down", we see many instances where Jesus had protection and escaped being murdered by angry men or crowds. [Matthew 2:13, Luke 4:29, John 8:59, 12:36]. Look up these protection scriptures: Luke 10:19, Mark 16:18, 2 Kings 6:17, Acts 9:23-25, Acts 27:22-24.

**#6 Action is Required**: Psalm 91 is not automatic, but lists some things for us to do. God offers us a place of refuge, but very clearly, our part of protection involves speaking our faith back to the Lord. Many times the problem lies in the area of not doing what the scripture tells us to do as our part. Abide in the shelter of the Almighty and don't wait until you are already under attack to start declaring the promises over your life.

**#7 It is Not Over Until it is Over!** Are there any promises for the situation after tragedy has struck? The one thing that I can tell you is that the Sovereignty of God is able to take the worst blow the devil has done to us and turn it around for good in our lives when we love Him and are called according to His service (Rom. 8:28). But there is a big difference in thinking *"all things are good"* versus *"God working all things out for good"*. What is meant for evil, God can work "or weave" for good if we believe Him to do it. (See Gen. 50: 20) So much good can come out of tragedy if we keep serving God and show our love for Him by taking His promises to us seriously. God brings so much good out of some situations that sometimes we mistakenly believe that He sent the evil.

Which one of these 7 things to remember "after tragedy has occurred" had you not thought about before? Which one most speaks to you?

# THE UNIQUE QUALITIES OF PSALM 91

Psalm 91 is a powerful gathering of the protection promises all in one chapter. The Psalm really speaks to intense situations such as war, accidents, fatal diseases, and those times when the world goes crazy—like the days in which we are living. There are promises throughout the Bible, but this is a unique and thorough collection of the very best. Although Psalm 91 doesn't address what to do in the case of something that has already gone wrong, please consider these questions.

*1. What did the character of Jesus tell us about God's view of life and death?*

*2. From your own knowledge of reading the Bible, when did death first enter into the picture?*

*3. What sort of actions can we take as preventative measures?*

*4. If something bad has already happened, is it too late for something good to come out of it?*

*5. Explain the difference between the concepts of protection from evil and martyrdom?*

*6. What other scriptures do you know that hold promise for protection and healing?*

*7. How does Psalm 91 hold a unique place among the protection promises?*

## OTHER RELATED VERSES

Revelation 12:11: *And they overcame him because of the blood of the Lamb and because of the word of their testimony, and they did not love their life even unto death.*

Psalm 118:17: *I shall not die, but live, and proclaim the works of the Lord.*

Revelation 3:10: *Because you have kept the word of My perseverance, I also will keep you from the hour of testing, that hour which is about to come upon the whole world....*

John 17:15: *I'm not asking you to take them out of the world, but protect them from the evil one.*

Matthew 6:13: [Pray then in this way:] *'Lead us away from temptation, and deliver us from evil.'*

# MAKE IT REAL: WHAT IS A LONG LIFE ? Psalm 91:14-16

### Life Connection Parable

Who in the Bible lived to be the oldest man on earth? _____ Genesis 5:27
How long did he live? _____ Genesis 5:27
What caused man to have his life-span shortened? _____
What does the Bible consider a long life? Genesis 6:3 _____ Psalm 90: 10 _____
   Worthy of Mention: **Deut. 34:7** Although 120, Moses eyes not dimmed or his vigor abated.
   Worthy of Mention: **Joshua 14:10-12** Caleb: Age 85 Give me this mountain!
Other Promises about a long life: I Kings 3:14, Ephesians 6:2-3, Proverb 10:27

In Dr. Reginald Cherry's book "The Bible Cure" it says: Scientists have been trying to unravel the mysteries of aging for decades. In the early fifties, Leonard Hayflick, a scientist at the University of California, San Francisco, discovered a very interesting thing: All human cells are able to reproduce themselves only a certain number of times. This is estimated to be about fifty cell divisions, which Dr. Hayflick estimated would place the human life at between one hundred fifteen and one hundred twenty years. Researchers still don't know what drives this cellular timetable, but the life span of humans seems to be set at approximately one hundred twenty years. Researchers can study a culture of human cells as they divide repeatedly until a maximum of fifty to sixty divisions, which equates to one hundred twenty years.

# MAKE IT MINE: HAPPY BIRTHDAY TO ME! HAPPY BIRTHDAY TO ME!

### Life Relevance Project

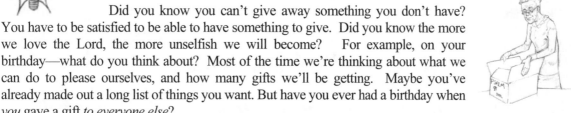

Did you know you can't give away something you don't have? You have to be satisfied to be able to have something to give. Did you know the more we love the Lord, the more unselfish we will become? For example, on your birthday—what do you think about? Most of the time we're thinking about what we can do to please ourselves, and how many gifts we'll be getting. Maybe you've already made out a long list of things you want. But have you ever had a birthday when *you* gave a gift *to everyone else*?

Last year a lady from Minnesota called me to say that she was going to have a birthday party to celebrate her hundredth birthday. She wanted to buy several hundred Psalm 91 books to give to each of her friends who came to her party. Most people would be thinking about the big party and all the gifts they would be getting—especially on their 100th birthday—but this lady was thinking about everyone else. That is a good example of someone who has lived a long, satisfied life—and you can't get that kind of satisfaction any other way, except by walking closely to Jesus.

**EXCERPT FROM PSALM 91 YOUTH BOOK**

## Satisfaction is Contagious

Matthew 10:8 encourages us that we should freely give what we have freely received!
Check what you have "freely received" in life and then fill out *an idea of how to give it*.

A Good Loving Childhood and Upbringing _____
Victory over some Area of Struggle _____
A Happy Marriage _____
Financial Blessings _____
Forgiveness _____
Extra Time _____
A Nice Vacation _____
Talents _____
A Good Background in Scripture _____
A Joyful Heart _____
A Healing _____
A Smile _____
Eternal Salvation _____
Other: _____

# Bible Interaction

List other Scriptures which relate to this chapter that come to mind.
John 10:10-Life and Life Abundantly, Proverbs 18:21-Life and Death in the Tongue,
Deuteronomy 30:19-Choose you this day life and the blessing

**Thought for Today:** Some people think that if they have seen something that did not work in someone else's life, they can't believe the promise for themselves. I challenge you to apply this positively: If you have ever seen a promise work in someone's life, even just once, apply that promise to your life!

Promises you have seen work in other people's lives: _____
_____
_____

**Link to Last Week**: Recount all the ways in which God has rescued you from trouble and honored you.

**Bait to Next Week:** Next week we will see how we can actually take hold of God's salvation: His health, healing, deliverance, protection and provision. Could there be some promises in His Word that we don't know about yet?

## *Respond With Your Heart*

*What does life and life more abundantly [John 10:10] mean to me?*
_____
_____

*Have I ever said, "I wish I could die!" Have I ever secretly hoped that I would accidentally die? If so, what can I do about it?* _____
_____
_____

*What are some areas I have deep satisfaction in? What are some areas that I lack satisfaction?*_____
_____
_____
_____

*Who do I know that has lived a life unto the Lord with great satisfaction?*_____
_____

# LESSON SIXTEEN: I BEHOLD HIS SALVATION!
## READ CHAPTER TWENTY ONE AND SUMMARY

Psalm 91:16b: "… and let him behold My salvation."

Kip came from a family that never had enough money. Daily living was a struggle. Travel, education and extras had never been a part of his growing-up years. However, there was one thing he wanted; it was to give the girl of his dreams the finest honeymoon ever. Carrie, his fiancé, had never traveled outside the state where she was born and she dreamed of going to some far-off, exotic place.

Since an early age, Kip loved the Lord and had served Him to the best of his ability. His relationship with Carrie reflected that love for the Lord. They had dated through his last year in high school and all the way through college. At last, the long awaited moment finally arrived. When Kip graduated from college, it was time to set the wedding date. Kip had saved money for his family's part in the wedding, but nothing seemed to be left over for the honeymoon. Kip prayed and Kip agonized. Then a big surprise happened. God had answered his prayer in a dramatic way. Kip's uncle said he didn't have a present for the bride and groom to unwrap at the ceremony, but he did have a card for them and it would arrive in the mail.

Kip and Carrie couldn't believe it was true as they sat on one of the most beautiful beaches in the world—two weeks in Hawaii. Kip couldn't have been more grateful for his uncle's wedding present. Carrie was thrilled beyond words and told Kip over and over. However, Kip had no money for extras. He scraped everything he could together to get passports (which they found out they didn't need). After three days they were eating sandwiches in their room. Almost a week and a half to go and no money for food!

At night they would sit on the pier watching other honeymooners enjoying luaus on the beach and listening to their laughter filling up the star lit night. If Carrie was disappointed, she never let Kip know it. They would pass by the dining hall and try not to look into where live bands were crooning the distinct native music to elegantly dressed couples dining by candlelight. They made everything they had stretch and took advantage of any public places within walking distance which they could go for entertainment. Day after day they watched as couples came off the beach with snorkeling gear in hand and stories galore of fish and shells and underwater wonders. It seemed like every night the restaurant served their guests *theme* dinners out under the stars, catered by a chef who cooked anything you wanted off the menu. The only time Carrie said an *"I wish…"* was the day when couples gathered in the hotel lobby to go on a picnic to another island and a friendly pair invited them to go along. The couple looked confused when Kip and Carrie made excuses.

Several unsuspected surprises happened where Kip and Carrie ran into people who needed help, but because they were barely getting by themselves, they had no resources to help: a stranded man who had run out of gas; a homeless person for whom Kip would normally have bought a hamburger; a woman with three small children who had been robbed in broad daylight. Kip felt foolish when he had to tell them that he honestly had no way of helping them. By the end of the week, Kip and Carrie had been out of funds for food for six days and had depleted every source of help they could think of.

Kip and Carrie had been taught to be thankful for what they had and they were grateful for their two weeks in paradise. What they weren't expecting when they got home was to find a handwritten note in plain sight from Kip's uncle. In the note he detailed every provision for their stay in Hawaii. They had received their e-tickets and the phone call, but the provision letter had slipped out of the card onto the dresser. There it was in black and white--an outline for their honeymoon. It was an all-inclusive trip. The uncle's letter had told them about the water sports, the snorkeling gear, the dining on the beaches, the food, the luau—and the island picnic! It had all been provided for, but Kip and Carrie didn't realize it. Kip's uncle had paid for not only the trip, but for every detail of the trip and Kip and Carrie did not know it until it was too late.

1. How does this story reflect the spiritual blessings God has provided for us beyond salvation?

2. How could Kip and Carrie's honeymoon have been different if they had known it was all inclusive?

3. Name any areas in your life where you can explore aspects of provision that you never have experienced.

This story gives us a good analogy of what it is like when we just understand salvation as merely being a ticket to heaven, rather than including all the provisions that come with it. A careful study of the word in both the Greek and Hebrew show a much more abundant life than what we generally think of when we think of the word salvation. Conventional theology and common interpretation has not explored what salvation really means. **Research the concept of salvation in the Bible**...

**Are there areas where you have not received the all-inclusive provision of your salvation much like Kip and Carrie?**

# MAKE IT MEANINGFUL:
### Life Application Questions

1. Write out the second half of Psalm 91:16 - _____

_____

2. What is the seventh promise?

3. What does the word *behold* mean?
4. What do most people think *salvation* means?

5. How does Strong's Concordance define salvation?

6. What other two ways can we take hold of the salvation this covenant provides?

7. What is the prayer of the author?

8. What is the truth about the protection, deliverance, health, and provision God provides?

---

The Greek word for "saved" and "salvation" is *sozo* and *soteria*. Most people think in terms of save and salvation to mean forgiveness of sins and regeneration, yet the word has a very rich meaning...

Other scriptures where these words are used. These are a few examples...

Luke 7:1-4, 10 ...Asking Him to come and (*dia-sozo*) the life of the slave...

Matthew 14:36 ...and as many as touched it were cured (*diasozo*).

Matthew 9:21-22 ...And at once the woman was (*sozo*).

Mark 5: 23 ...lay your hands on her, that she may get well (*sozo*) and live.

Luke 8:36 ...how the man who was demon-possessed had been (*sozo*)...

Acts 4: 9 ...if we are on trial today for a benefit done to a sick man, as to how this man has been (*sozo*).

James 5:15... the prayer offered in faith will (*sozo*) the one who is sick, the Lord will raise him up...

**In this list there is an example of healing, deliverance, raising the dead, etc. Scripture continues the concept of (sozo) passing to the disciples in Acts and on to the instructions James gave to the church.**

---

**The definition for *salvation* is rich in meaning. Look up the word in the Greek and Hebrew to see how much more that word salvation promises by definition.**

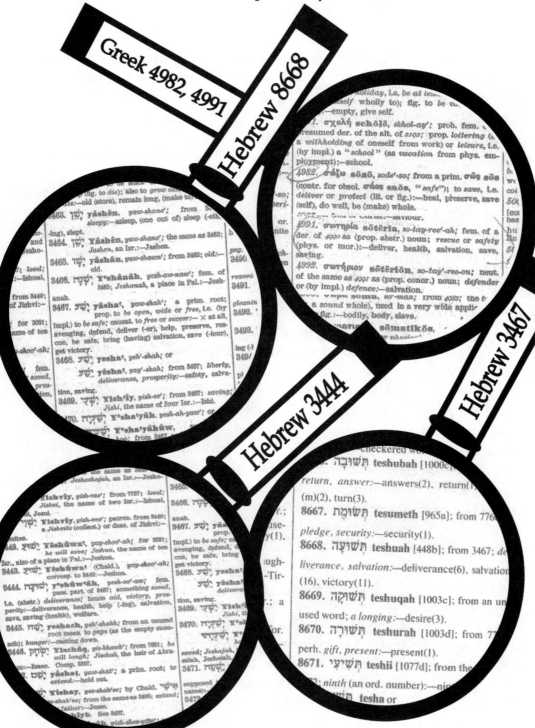

# MAKE IT REAL: WEAVED TOGETHER FOR GOOD
Life Connection Parable

I started this Psalm 91 study by telling about my father and the fishing trips he took us on as we grew up. I told about his unexpected death. **Now, I would like to end this chapter by telling about his life.** My dad came from a divorced home and lived with his grandparents who had very little money, so he didn't have anything except the bare necessities. By the time he was six he was on the streets selling newspapers to buy his school clothes.

There was certainly no money for pets, but one day his grandfather caught a little, wild bunny rabbit and gave it to him to bottle feed. Dad loved that rabbit and carried it with him everywhere he went. One day, with his little rabbit in his arms, he ran and jumped on his bed, not realizing that his weight was going to break the rabbit's neck. That sad experience was probably why he always wanted animals around when he was grown and why he made sure all the grandchildren had pets. Often we would catch him putting a grandbaby, still in diapers, on the back of one of his goats. As we got older, riding that goat while holding onto its horns was more fun than a carousel.

In high school dad became the city boxing champion and held that title until someone secretly brought in a professional boxer who took Dad down. The newspaper had a picture of my dad, the town champion, knocked out and lying flat on his back. The headlines read, *"The Mighty Crow Has Fallen."*

Dad was the star player on his Howard Payne College football team. I read newspaper articles my mother had pasted in her scrapbook that called Dad *The Tank*. One article said, "Crow looked like an army tank going through a corn field, mowing down everything in its pathway." Dad's football years were before extreme hazing was outlawed, so he went through some really tough punishment. I've heard him talk about the belt lines where they were told to strip down and carry a torch in the dark while being made to run between two lines of older football players who popped them with belts as they ran past. Dad was good at what he did. He was even offered a contract to play for the Green Bay Packers, but he turned it down to marry my mother during his last year at college. He served in World War II and then came home to a loving wife and raised three children who adored him. He became the father to his children that he always wished he had.

God was abundantly blessing him, but something was missing. He was such a good man with Godly morals that I didn't realize while I was living at home that **he had not yet seen His Salvation!** You can imagine the surprise and joy I felt the day he called, asking me to come to his baptism that night. And what a difference it made! He had always been a good, loving person; but from that day forward, his entire life changed. He would witness about Jesus to everyone he met, take food to people on his mail route who were in need, repair mail boxes for the elderly, slip candy to the children… He loved God with his whole heart, soul, mind and strength, and he didn't mind the world knowing it. When he went home to be with the Lord, his Bible told the story of his new life because it was covered with highlighted passages and notes in the margins— painting a picture of the *love walk* that he enjoyed with his heavenly Father. **He had indeed SEEN THE SALVATION OF THE LORD.**

#1 Has God brought good out of something meant for evil in my life?

#2 Is there an area that still causes pain that I could believe the promise that God is able to bring something good out of the tragedy?

#3 How can you make the most of your days?

Think of different areas in your life where the devil has stolen your blessings, all the way through the spectrum of your life to areas where you are living in abundance. Remember the covenant God has provided, and remind the devil he can't steal your blessings! Circle the step you most often find yourself on. Different areas of your life may be on different steps.

## VICTORY AND KINGDOM-MINDED LIVING

Living in the promises

Being blessed to be
a blessing

Praying for others as well as ourselves

Having a "love walk" with the Lord

Actively bringing God's involvement
into all areas of life

Pray about the
big decisions and needs in life
but not the day to day details

Knowledge that blessings
are available but never
pressing in

Not knowing promises
are available in the Bible

If anything good happens,
something goes wrong

Lazy Passive Christian

"I won't bother God if
He won't bother me!"

If it can go wrong...
it happens to me.

## CALAMITY AND CRISIS LIVING

*Talk/Write about an experience where you didn't know about something and you lost out like Kip and Carrie. Talk/Write about an experience where someone passed on where you did receive an inheritance of some kind.* **DISCUSS YOUR REMEMBRANCES AS A GROUP.**

# MAKE IT MINE: MAKING GOOD USE OF THE PROMISES
### Life Relevance Project

*My grandparents lived through the Great Depression and I often heard them tell how they utilized everything on the farm. I remember hearing my children tell me about a visit they had with my grandmother and drinking milk from her refrigerator that had a long overdue expiration date. When she poured it into the glass the milk came out in chunks. The kids thought that it would kill her if she drank it, but she only laughed. She had been drinking it that way for years. I guess it couldn't have caused too much damage, she never went to the hospital, never took pills and lived into her nineties— one of the happiest women you would ever meet. This generation made a lifestyle out of wasting nothing and taught their children: Waste Not, Want Not. I could see in my parents, who had learned to live this way, the implications of this kind of an upbringing from their parents. Our family car was kept immaculate and in perfect running order. Our home was cared for as if it had been a castle. We learned as a family to make good use of what God had given us.*

Can you imagine a town where no one used what they had been given? They would have a very short existence: the people in the city had cars but once they ran out of gas, they just parked them. They didn't know what made the cars run. The people ate the food they could see, but did not know what to do to get more. The people neither married, nor had a concept of raising a family—they just lived as individuals. They had water, but did not know to drink it. The list could go on, but you get the point. Abundant provision could be all around and people could, for one reason or another, not know to utilize it. In your life, what part of the definition of salvation is not a reality in your experience?

**Your group is a team of writers and designers** who are designing a board game, or writing a skit or short TV or radio drama about a person, a town, country or church that does not utilize what they've been given. For example if you used themes in this chapter such as: characters who don't know what salvation means, characters who don't utilize the Psalm 91 covenant or promises from God's word, etc. It will add drama to your production to see all the things that go wrong when people don't utilize available resources. Don't forget to tie in at the end how this relates to a person who never utilizes what God has provided.

# Bible Interaction

List other Scriptures which relate to this chapter that come to mind.
John 10:10

**MEDITATE ON THE MEANING OF** Psalm 103:1—Bless the Lord, O my soul;
And all that is within me, bless His holy name. Bless the Lord, O my soul,
And forget none of His benefits... (and then it names the benefits)
List those benefits: _____

_____

_____

**Link to Last Week**: Recount all the ways in which God has rescued, honored and satisfied you with good things!

**Bait for the Rest of Your Days:** Seek ye first the Kingdom of God and His righteousness and all these things will be added to you. Matthew 6: 33.

## *Respond With Your Heart*

*What does salvation mean to me?* _____

_____

_____

*How can I lead more people to the Lord and into a deeper understanding of their covenant of salvation?* _____

_____

_____

*What are some benefits of Psalm 91 that I might not be walking in?*

_____

_____

*What is the benefit package promised us from the word salvation?*

_____

_____

_____

# Journal

# SUMMARY

1. Nothing in this world can be relied upon as confidently as God's promises when
_____,
_____
_____.

2. Why should we believe that one can take a song from the psalms and base his life on it?




3. Because Jesus saw the Psalms, the Law of Moses and the Prophets as equally inspired (Luke 24: 44), what should that tell us?




4. What is comforting to know in these uncertain times?

# Call 91-1

# SOME OF YOU ENJOY A GOOD CROSSWORD PUZZLE. TRY THIS ONE OUT!

Across

1 A defensive wall; fortified rampart
2 Messengers of God
3 As a result of this or that; consequently
4 To disturb or agitate
5 Either of the two four limbs of a bird
6 In accordance with justice, law and morality
7 To stay, remain, reside
8 The person to whom one is speaking
9 Period of light between sunrise and sunset
10 A feather; a wing
11 The quality of being worthy of trust; able to be relied
12 One with great power and authority; Master
13 Intense fear; a person or thing that causes intense fe
14 Morally bad; wicked
15 All powerful, God, the Lord
16 Opposite of against
17 Shelter or protection from danger
18 Lower than; below
19 Level; not irregular
20 To free or save from danger
21 Opposite of old
22 To place something over so as to hide
23 The act or process of destroying
24 To crush; to destroy
25 Serpent
26 Causing death, fatal
27 To remain, to stand fast, to reside
28 To swell, increase; ten hundred
29 Where 10,000 may fall (2 words; backwards)
30 King of the jungle (plural)

Down

1 To happen; come to pass
2 Felling fear; frightened
3 Place of safety
4 Firm belief or confidence in another pe
5 A broad piece of protective armor carr
6 To operate in security
7 Ephesians 6:2-3: for obedience promi
(Opposite of premature death)
8 High regard or great respect given
9 To set free or save from evil
10 Any fatal disease
11 A fortified place, fort
12 Organs of sight
13 One who traps
14 An image that is worshipped, Deity
15 To make repayment
16 To keep safe from harm
17 A kind of trap
18 To walk on or to walk over
19 A definite area of shade made by one'
20 A saving or being saved: preservation
21 Anything that afflicts or troubles; calar
22 Having regard to
23 _ _ _ _ _ _ - slayer
24 Opposite of day
25 To have had a clear perception or kno
26 Relatively close in distance
27 Male gender pronoun

148

# TESTIMONY SECTION

## Extra Credit:

1. Take each testimony in the back of your Psalm 91 book and see how the individual or someone else in the story applied Psalm 91.

2. Write up the different types of miracles of protection this person witnessed.

## Assignment:

3. Write your own personal Psalm 91 testimony from an experience that happened in your life.

### Example: Jake Weise Testimony, Infantry Machine-gunner, Corporal, Marines (excerpt)

During the time I was in Iraq, I always felt protected. This was largely due to the fact that before I left for boot-camp, I had been taught and had taken hold of one thing—the 91st Psalm and the power and promises contained in its verses that protect us from every form of evil that the enemy tries to bring against us.

While I was a college student and in the delayed entry program waiting to go to boot-camp, Peggy Joyce taught us one of the most thorough and complete breakdowns of scripture I had ever heard. I normally don't retain all that much out of a message or a sermon, but her teaching on the 91st Psalm and how to apply it to our lives burned itself into my soul. I really had never realized just how much power the words of that psalm held. I remembered it and have since applied it to my life. I believe with all my heart that standing on that word brought me through my deployments without a scratch physically *or* spiritually.

On June 24, 2004, my company had been holding off small arms, mortar, and RPG fire, but the fire intensified to an insane level—an approximate six-to-seven-hour exchange of fire. I had never been under that intense a barrage of fire before. It was crazy how I felt right then. I can't really describe it. I just remember praying the whole time I was out there. Without stopping, I was praying in the spirit and praying the 91st Psalm over us....

At that point we had taken seven casualties, five from our Company, and two from the supporting units that responded. Even the circumstances of those Marines' wounds were miraculous in nature and we didn't have a single KIA. Sniper fire had resulted in two of our Marines, including our Company Commander, being shot in the head. In both cases, however, the bullets had not penetrated the bone. They left only an ugly gash (flesh wound) where the bullet traveled along the skull....

Over the next week, almost daily we exchanged fire with insurgents. One more Marine took an identical sniper shot to the head and it did not enter his skull. You can't call surviving a hit with a .50 cal—and recovering fully—anything *but* miraculous.

The most important part of all this is the fact that during the entire fire fight, the 91st Psalm rolled through my head. I never felt like anything ever came remotely close to me. In April, I had a mortar round hit so close that it killed the Marine in front of me and wounded two others around us, but I didn't feel so much as shrapnel go by me. Truly, men fell to my right and left, *but it didn't come near me* (Psalm 91: 7). Please take it to heart. It will save your life and the lives of others.

# EPILOGUE:

*Do you remember Jennifer at the beginning of the workbook? What ever happened to her? Did she face a time in Africa when she needed Psalm 91? Here is the rest of her story...*

"I lived in a village in the bush with the Ankole tribe (cattle herders), working with orphans with AIDS and teaching at the village school. I often found myself praying Psalm 91 while walking the circumference of the village. But I had no idea of the power in this passage until January 15, 2000. I had gone to the city the day before on the milk truck. That night I was lying in my hut and heard gunshots.

I ran into a fellow missionary's hut and knelt on my knees in a small room praying Psalm 91 over and over. The missionary was out investigating, so it was just his 24-year-old wife, their 2-year-old child and me.

In the meantime, a group of rebels were raiding my village. Men in our village were killed, a pregnant woman beaten, the village was robbed and cattle were stolen. The villagers were laid out in a line on their stomachs with guns and machetes pointed to their heads, while they were being ordered not to say a word. The raid was well planned, as the rebels had been watching us for days from the bushes.

Here is the miracle! Village people know that white missionaries have more in their huts than Ugandans make in a lifetime. Yet the rebels never came to our hut—in spite of the fact that everyone else's hut was raided. Afterward, the rebels admitted to the police that they had followed the milk truck through the bush the night before the raid. I had been on that truck, sitting right next to the driver who was carrying two million shillings - the villagers' monthly income from the milk sales. They did not attack the truck en route because we had returned home before dark that night. This was the first time we had ever returned before dark in the six months I had been riding it.

The day after the attack was very intense. I walked through the village praying for villagers who had been robbed and beaten. They had looks of pure terror on their faces, knowing that the rebels were still hiding in the bush nearby. When I talked to the villagers, no one could believe that I was not attacked. My interpreter, Segambe, said, "It was as if your hut was not even there."

God did not give Psalm 91 only to missionaries in the African bush. He gave it to everyone so that we can daily claim His promises to us as Christians. I'm going to have to thank Donna for impressing upon me the power of this psalm!"

**Some of you are planning to be missionaries. Some of you are in the military, some of you are fighting life threatening situations—and you've never studied this psalm. Borrowing from the words of Donna: "I don't hate you, I love you"—that's why I'm telling you—"Get this psalm inside of you!"**

**P. J. Ruth**

# PSALM 91

**For Him:**

1 He who dwells in the shelter of the Most High
   Will abide in the shadow of the Almighty.
2 I will say to the Lord, "My refuge and my fortress,
   My God, in whom I trust!"
3 For it is He who delivers you from the snare of the trapper
   And from the deadly pestilence.
4 He will cover you with His pinions,
   And under His wings you may seek refuge;
   His faithfulness is a shield and bulwark.

5 You will not be afraid of the terror by night,
   Or of the arrow that flies by day;
6 Of the pestilence that stalks in darkness,
   Or of the destruction that lays waste at noon.
7 A thousand may fall at your side,
   And ten thousand at your right hand;
   But it shall not approach you.
8 You will only look on with your eyes,
   And see the recompense of the wicked.
9 For you have made the Lord, my refuge,
   Even the Most High, your dwelling place.
10 No evil will befall you,
   Nor will any plague come near your tent.

11 For He will give His angels charge concerning you,
   To guard you in all your ways.
12 They will bear you up in their hands,
   Lest you strike your foot against a stone.
13 You will tread upon the lion and cobra,
   The young lion and the dragon you will trample down.

14 "Because _____ has loved Me, therefore I will deliver him;
   I will set him securely on high, because he has known My name.
15 He will call upon Me, and I will answer him;
   I will be with him in trouble;
   I will rescue him, and honor him.
16 With a long life I will satisfy him,
   And let him behold my salvation.

# PSALM 91

**For Her:**

1 He who dwells in the shelter of the Most High
   Will abide in the shadow of the Almighty.
2 I will say to the Lord, "My refuge and my fortress,
   My God, in whom I trust!"
3 For it is He who delivers you from the snare of the trapper
   And from the deadly pestilence.
4 He will cover you with His pinions,
   And under His wings you may seek refuge;
   His faithfulness is a shield and bulwark.

5 You will not be afraid of the terror by night,
   Or of the arrow that flies by day;
6 Of the pestilence that stalks in darkness,
   Of of the destruction that lays waste at noon.
7 A thousand may fall at your side,
   And ten thousand at your right hand;
   But it shall not approach you.
   And see the recompense of the wicked.
8 You will only look on with your eyes,
9 For you have made the Lord, my refuge,
   Even the Most High, your dwelling place.
10 No evil will befall you,
   Nor will any plague come near your tent.

11 For He will give His angels charge concerning you,
   To guard you in all your ways.
12 They will bear you up in their hands,
   Lest you strike your foot against a stone.
13 You will tread upon the lion and cobra,
   The young lion and the dragon you will trample down.

14 "Because _____ has loved Me, therefore I will deliver her;
   I will set her securely on high, because she has known My name.
15 She will call upon Me, and I will answer her;
   I will be with her in trouble;
   I will rescue her, and honor her.
16 With a long life I will satisfy her,
   And let her behold My salvation."

# PRAYER of COMMITMENT

Dear God:

I believe You gave your Son, Jesus, to die for me. I believe He shed His Blood to pay for my sins and that You raised Him from the dead so I can be Your child and live with You eternally in heaven. I am asking Jesus to come into my heart right now and save me. I confess Him as the Lord and Master of my life.

I thank You, dear Lord, for loving me enough to lay down your life for me. Take my life now and use it for Your Glory. I ask for all that You have for me.

In Jesus Name,

Amen

# Evaluate Your Workbook Experience

I completed the workbook as:   ○ an individual   ○ in a group study

(If in a group study, check one below)

○ Men's Bible Study   ○ Ladies Bible Study   ○ Military Chaplain Bible Study
○ Sunday School  ○ Prison Chaplaincy program   ○ Youth Group  ○ Other_____

How did you find out about the Psalm 91 Workbook? _____

_____

This workbook…       ○       Provided a new understanding of my covenant of protection.

                             ○       Revived my existing understanding of my covenant of protection.

                             ○       Helped me in other areas of my spiritual growth.

    ○  Other: _____

Please describe how this workbook helped you:

_____

_____

_____

How can we improve this workbook?

_____

_____

_____

Do you have any Psalm 91 testimonies that you would like to share? _____

_____

_____

_____

Thank you for your response!  Please remove this page and mail your completed form to:

Peggy Joyce Ruth Ministries P.O. Box 1549, Brownwood, TX 76804

www.peggyjoyceruth.org

Please provide contact information if you send a testimony:

Name _____Email _____   Phone _____

Address _____

# OTHER BOOKS AVAILABLE

 PSALM 91: God's Umbrella of Protection (for Adults)

 Psalm 91: God's Umbrella of Protection (for Youth)

 My Own Psalm 91 Book (Young Children and Toddlers)
Board Book with Full Color Illustrations

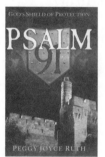 Psalm 91: God's Shield of Protection (Expanded Edition: Military, Firemen, Policemen, Prison Guards) Hardback & Paperback

Those Who Trust the Lord Shall Not be Disappointed

Tormented: Eight Years and Back

   (Testimony and Spiritual Warfare Handbook)

God's Smuggler, Jr.

      (Testimony on Smuggling Bibles into China)

      by Peggy Joyce Ruth's daughter, Angelia Schum

# HEAR PEGGY JOYCE !!!!

To LISTEN to this **audio message** by
Peggy Joyce Ruth,
*Those Who Trust in the Lord*
*Shall Not Be Disappointed*
as well as other teachings including
*Psalm 91*
*Peggy Joyce's Testimony,*
please visit
www.peggyjoyceruth.org

All of her teachings may be downloaded
for your own personal use.

Details of Streaming Audio available on Website
www.peggyjoyceruth.org
Peggy Joyce's & Angelia Schum's Radio Broadcasts
KPSM 99.3 & KBUB 90.3 FM

Downloads available
Angelia Ruth Schum
www.crosslines.net